Road to the Code

Road to the Code

A Phonological Awareness Program for Young Children

by

Benita A. Blachman, Ph.D.
Syracuse University, New York

Eileen Wynne Ball, Ph.D.
University of Illinois at Chicago

Rochella Black, M.S.
Syracuse City School District, New York
Northport–East Northport School District, New York

Darlene M. Tangel, Ph.D.
Syracuse University, New York
Oriskany Central School District, New York

·PAUL·H·
BROOKES
PUBLISHING Cº. ®

Baltimore • London • Sydney

Paul H. Brookes Publishing Co.
Post Office Box 10624
Baltimore, Maryland 21285-0624
www.brookespublishing.com

Typeset by Barton Matheson Willse & Worthington, Baltimore, Maryland.
Manufactured in the United States of America by
Bang Printing, Brainerd, Minnesota.

Supported by a grant from the National Center for Learning Disabilities, 381 Park Avenue South, Suite 1401, New York, NY 10016.

The illustrations in the front matter and the text are courtesy of Eric Howes.

The illustrations in the alphabet picture cards, sound categorization cards, and Elkonin cards are courtesy of Mindy Ball Oswald.

Permission is gratefully acknowledged to reprint the following jingle:
ONE OF THESE THINGS
Music: Joe Raposo
Words: Bruce Hart
© 1970 Jonico Music, Inc.
Copyright renewed.
Rights in the U.S.A. administered by Stage Harbor Publishing Inc.

Third printing, April 2010.

Library of Congress Cataloging-in-Publication Data
Road to the code : a phonological awareness program for young children /
   by Benita A. Blachman . . . [et al.].
       p.   cm.
     Includes bibliographical references (p.).
     ISBN-13: 978-1-55766-438-9
     ISBN-10: 1-55766-438-2
     1. Children—Language.   2. English language—Phonetics—Study and teaching (Early childhood).   3. Reading—Phonetic method.   4. Language awareness in children.
   I. Blachman, Benita A.
   LB1139.L3 R54   2000
   372.46'5—dc21   99-055299

British Library Cataloguing-in-Publication data are available from the British Library

Contents

Contents

About the Authors

Benita A. Blachman, Ph.D., Professor, School of Education, Syracuse University, Syracuse, New York

Benita A. Blachman is a professor in the Reading and Language Arts Department and Coordinator of the Graduate Program in Learning Disabilities in the School of Education at Syracuse University. She also holds a courtesy appointment in the Communication Sciences and Disorders Department. She has a doctoral degree in educational psychology from the University of Connecticut and is a former special education teacher, reading specialist, and learning disabilities consultant. She has published extensively in the area of early literacy, focusing her research on early intervention to prevent reading failure and on the factors that predict reading achievement. Dr. Blachman is currently directing a project at Syracuse University (in collaboration with researchers at Yale Medical School and the University of Texas–Houston Health Science Center) funded by the National Institute of Child Health and Human Development to investigate the influence of intensive reading intervention on patterns of brain activation in young children. Dr. Blachman has served on the professional advisory boards of the National Center for Learning Disabilities, the National Dyslexia Research Foundation, and the Neuhaus Center. Her edited book *Foundations of Reading Acquisition and Dyslexia: Implications for Early Intervention* was published recently by Lawrence Erlbaum Associates.

Eileen Wynne Ball, Ph.D., Associate Professor, College of Education, University of Illinois at Chicago, Illinois, and Third-Grade Teacher, Public School District 36, Winnetka, Illinois

Eileen Wynne Ball is an associate professor in the College of Education at the University of Illinois at Chicago (UIC), where she was the recipient of two major teaching awards. She has a doctoral degree in education from Syracuse University, where she also earned a master's degree in urban education. Before joining the faculty of the UIC, Dr. Ball received a second master's degree from Northeastern Illinois University and taught at Barat College in Lake Forest, Illinois; she also taught at Le Moyne College in Syracuse, New York, where she created and coordinated Le Moyne's program for special education teachers. Prior to her university work, Dr. Ball was an urban classroom teacher for 12 years. In Chicago, she directed and

About the Authors

taught in The Parents School, an early model in alternative urban education, and she continues to do educational consulting nationally. Her research in phonological awareness has won her grants and fellowships from the National Dyslexia Research Association, the U.S. Department of Education, Office of Special Education and Rehabilitative Services, and the Spencer Foundation. Dr. Ball is returning to UIC after completing another 2 years as a full-time third-grade classroom teacher during which she deepened her belief that classroom practices and classroom teachers must inform educational research.

Rochella Black, M.S., Learning Disabilities and Early Childhood Specialist, formerly of the Syracuse City School District, Syracuse, New York, and the Northport–East Northport School Disctrict, Northport, New York

Rochella Black has been a kindergarten teacher, first-grade teacher, and special education resource teacher for 24 years, teaching in both the inner-city schools of Syracuse, New York, and the suburban schools in Northport-East Northport, New York. Over the years, she has also served as a private tutor for students of all ages who were experiencing difficulty learning to read. In addition, Ms. Black was the project coordinator of the large-scale kindergarten and first-grade reading research project directed by Dr. Blachman during which the *Road to the Code* manual was developed and evaluated. She has presented numerous seminars and in-service courses for teachers on the effectiveness of specific activities for developing phonological awareness in children at the beginning stages of reading. She holds an undergraduate degree from the University of Michigan in social studies and two master's degrees from Syracuse University in elementary education and special education with a specialization in learning disabilities. Her publications have appeared in *Reading and Writing: An Interdisciplinary Journal.*

Darlene M. Tangel, Ph.D., Reading Specialist and Chairperson, Committee on Special Education, Oriskany Central School District, Oriskany, New York, and Adjunct Assistant Professor, School of Education, Syracuse University, Syracuse, New York

Darlene M. Tangel is an adjunct assistant professor in the Reading and Language Arts Department at Syracuse University. She has taught graduate courses in learning disabilities and in language disorders at Syracuse

University and has been a reading specialist in the Oriskany Public Schools for more than 20 years, where she also serves as the Chair of Special Education and the Chair of Preschool Special Education. Her research interests include early reading acquisition and invented spelling, alternative reading curricula for children at risk for reading failure, and adult literacy. She has developed training materials for the American Federation of Teachers and has extensive experience conducting teacher training workshops. The focus of these workshops is translating research into practical application for classroom use. Her most recent publications have appeared in the *Journal of Reading Behavior* and *Reading and Writing: An Interdisciplinary Journal*. Drs. Tangel and Blachman were awarded the Dina Feitelson Research Award by the International Reading Association for their research on invented spelling.

Preface and Acknowledgments

This manual is the culmination of a project that has been in the works for more than 10 years. In an early study (Blachman, 1987), I worked with first-grade teachers to create an alternative reading program for children who were having difficulty learning to read. We started by developing activities to heighten phonological awareness—for example, using Elkonin cards to develop phoneme segmentation skills. It became clear from the research that we should be introducing activities to enhance phonological awareness even earlier, and that meant creating activities for kindergarten teachers.

For our first kindergarten study (Ball & Blachman, 1988, 1991), Eileen Wynne Ball developed many of the activities in this manual, including *Say-It-and-Move-It* (based on the work of Elkonin, 1973). Mindy Ball Oswald, an illustrator, designed many of the materials, specifically the alphabet picture cards, the sound categorization cards, and the Elkonin cards.

Over the years, the lessons were modified and expanded from 28 to more than 40, some of the original materials were modified, new materials were developed, and the program was evaluated in a second study (Blachman, Ball, Black, & Tangel, 1994; Tangel & Blachman, 1992, 1995). In the second study, kindergarten teachers and their classroom teaching assistants (rather than specially trained researchers) demonstrated that these phonological awareness activities could be used successfully with small groups of children in their classrooms. In the second half of the kindergarten year, children who could not yet read and who knew few, if any, letter sounds used this program, followed by a reading program in Grade 1 (and Grade 2, if necessary) that emphasized the alphabetic code. Children who participated in this program were better readers at the end of Grades 1 and 2 than similar children who did not participate in phonological awareness instruction in kindergarten (Blachman, Tangel, Ball, Black, & McGraw, 1999).

A few years ago, I was fortunate to receive a grant from the National Center for Learning Disabilities to adapt our research-based phonological awareness program and create a manual that could be used by teachers in a variety of settings. Although we developed this program with kinder-

Preface and Acknowledgments

garten children in mind, it has been used successfully with first graders who were struggling to learn to read. Teachers have introduced this program at different points during the year, depending on the needs of the children.

Many wonderful teachers have provided valuable feedback and assistance and have suggested revisions, and we especially want to thank Andi Alexander, Jennifer Bowers, Sheryl Cardone, Earlyne Hastings, Eric Howes, Rachel Karchmer, Jennifer McMaster, Marilyn Skopek, and Stacey White, as well as psychologists Dr. Julie Blumsak and Dr. Sheila Clonan.

We also want to thank several outstanding artists: Mindy Ball Oswald, Eric Howes, and Jennifer McMaster. As indicated earlier, Mindy Ball Oswald designed many of the original materials, with recent modifications made by Jennifer McMaster. Eric Howes is responsible for the drawings in the Introduction, Teacher Notes, and Lessons. (Corel Clipart was used for all of the pictures on our Sound Bingo cards. The jingle "One of These Things" is used with the permission of Jonico Music, Inc.) Eric and Susan Howes are also responsible for the title.

We also want to express our appreciation to the Office of Professional Development (OPD) at Syracuse University, directed by Dr. Scott Shablak, for technical assistance and help with the editing, production, and distribution of an earlier, prepublication version of this manual. The expert assistance of OPD staff members Michael Hardt and Christa Foster was invaluable.

Finally, our heartfelt thanks go to Elaine Niefeld, Lisa Rapisarda, Havely Taylor, and the entire staff at Paul H. Brookes Publishing Company for their unwavering support and assistance.

Benita A. Blachman
Syracuse, New York

Introduction

What Is Phonological Awareness?

esearchers and practitioners have clearly and consistently identified phonological awareness as a critical factor in learning to read. What is it, and why should it play such an important role in beginning reading? Simply stated, phonological awareness is an awareness of the phonological segments in speech—the segments of speech that are more or less represented by the letters of the alphabet. Research has shown that without this awareness, it is difficult to understand how an alphabet works—that is, how an alphabet transcribes speech. If children are not aware that the spoken word "sun," for example, has three segments, they won't be able to understand why *sun* is written with three letters.

What Makes Phonological Awareness Difficult?

Although the relationship between speech and print may seem obvious to adults, the relationship is far from obvious to many beginning readers. To understand the link between speech and print, the child must become aware that speech can be segmented into words, into syllables, and finally into even smaller units called phonemes. It is these phonemic units of speech that are represented in print. Explicit awareness that speech can be segmented into phonemic units, however, is not a natural byproduct of learning to speak. In fact, becoming consciously aware of these smaller linguistic units is only necessary when learning to read. Researchers now know that failure to develop this awareness is a major stumbling block in reading acquisition.

It is important for teachers of young beginning readers to realize that although the three segments of the written word *bag,* for example, can be easily identified, the three segments of the spoken word are not as obvious. This is because the segments of the spoken word are merged or coarticulated (i.e., the consonants are folded into the vowels) when we speak. As Isabelle Liberman and Donald Shankweiler explained:

> Though the word "bag," for example, has three phonological units, and, correspondingly, three letters in print, it has only one pulse of

Introduction

sound: The three elements of the underlying phonological structure—the three phonemes—have been thoroughly overlapped and merged into that one sound—"bag." (1991, p. 6)

Thus, to help children understand how an alphabet represents speech, it is often necessary to help them understand first that spoken words can be segmented into the phonemic units that the alphabet represents.

What Makes Learning to Read Difficult?

In trying to determine the source of the difficulty for many poor readers, researchers have asked children to demonstrate phonological awareness. For example, children have been asked to:

- Group words on the basis of common sounds (e.g., *pen* and *hen* go together because they rhyme; *hat* and *hen* go together because they begin with the same sound)

- Move disks to represent the sounds in simple words, such as *up* and *fan*

- Delete sounds from words (e.g., say "sat" without the /s/)

Research has shown that children who lack this level of phonological awareness, as demonstrated on one or more of these tasks, are likely to be among our poorest readers. Without phonological awareness, as we've said, the systematic relationships between print and speech are difficult to grasp, and this leads to poor decoding skills. It is our poor decoders, unfortunately, who fail to develop the word reading accuracy and fluency needed to support good reading comprehension.

Can Phonological Awareness Be Taught?

The good news is that teachers can enhance the development of phonological awareness. Large-scale training studies, both here and abroad, have found that instruction in phonological awareness facilitates beginning reading and spelling. When connections are made between the phonological segments in words and the letters representing those segments, the instruction is even more effective. We have known for some time that "the evidence is compelling: Toward the goal of efficient and effective reading instruction, explicit training of phoneme awareness is invaluable" (Adams, 1990, p. 331). Unfortunately, despite the evidence, activities to build phonological awareness have not routinely been integrated into our kindergarten and first-grade classrooms.

The program you are about to use in your classroom was developed to enable classroom teachers, resource and reading teachers, and language specialists to incorporate phonological awareness activities into the curriculum before children have had a chance to fail. The activities have been evaluated in systematic research with kindergarten and first-grade children who could not read and who knew few, if any, letter sounds. This program was found to be effective in enhancing beginning reading and spelling abilities for these children.

Is Phonological Awareness Enough?

It is important to remember that although activities to develop phonological awareness are a critical ingredient in fostering literacy acquisition, no one would suggest that these activities are all that is needed. Ideally, one would want phonological awareness activities to be incorporated into a classroom where reading to children is commonplace, oral language experiences are valued, basic concepts about print (e.g., how to hold a book) and the functions of reading and writing are developed, and children have opportunities both to talk and to write about their experiences. Within a rich oral and written language environment, we know that many children develop phonological awareness on their own by playing oral language games, by connecting speech and print when being read to, and by opportunities to write. Other children, however, are not so fortunate. Some children do not develop phonological awareness because they lack the early literacy experiences that often trigger this awareness. Still other children do not develop phonological awareness on their own, even with an abun-

Introduction

dance of preschool literacy experiences and opportunities to play with language, because they have differences or deficiencies in phonological ability. For these two groups of children especially, a systematic program to heighten phonological awareness is particularly important.

Can This Program Be Adapted to Meet Individual Needs?

To accommodate the individual differences one expects in a typical classroom, all of the activities in this program can be used easily with heterogeneous groups of children. As you read through the manual, you will be given specific examples of how activities can be made more challenging for some, while providing repetition and review at a more basic level for others in the same group. By making sure that all children develop the phonological awareness needed to understand how print represents speech, we can increase the likelihood that more of our children will be successful as they learn to read and spell.

A Word About Pacing

One of the most important factors contributing to the success of students using this program is proper pacing—the speed with which you move the group, and individual children within the group, through these lessons. Optimal pacing requires a delicate balance among activities that are challenging but not frustrating. In addition, if the pacing is appropriate, each child will be able to demonstrate a high rate of correct responses. It is important to remember, however, that within a group, not all children will be able to demonstrate a high rate of correct responses if questions are asked at only one level. To ensure success, expectations may need to differ for each child. In the Teacher Notes of this manual, we provide suggestions to help you modify the pacing of the lessons for individual children.

The main goal for children who are beginning this program is fairly simple. They need to develop the awareness that spoken words can be segmented into phonemes and that these segmented units can be represented by the

Introduction

letters of the alphabet. If we want children to be successful, we need to recognize that some children take longer than others to develop this level of phonological awareness. Phonological awareness unfolds gradually over time and continues to develop as children learn to read.

We encourage you to use your best judgment regarding pacing decisions. For example, although in our research we used this program over an 11-week period and provided small groups of four or five kindergarten children with four 15- to 20-minute lessons per week, that may not be appropriate in your classroom. Depending on the skill level of your children, you may find that you need more than 11 weeks to introduce these concepts, or you may find that you can move more quickly than we suggest.

The sequence of skills to be introduced will generally be the same across children; however, the number of lessons actually needed to master each skill may vary. For some children, it will be appropriate to follow the lessons as described, while others may need many more lessons to develop the same level of understanding. It is very appropriate to repeat a lesson (or even to conduct the identical lesson 2 or more days in a row), if that is what your students need. Some children may develop the ability to segment two-phoneme items relatively quickly, for example. In that case, you could skip some of the lessons that we

Introduction

have devoted to that concept and go on to three-phoneme segmentation. Other children may need more than double the number of lessons devoted to two-phoneme segmentation to achieve competence in that skill. Don't read these lessons as an unalterable script. Proper pacing is crucial.

Proper pacing is crucial!

Some Prerequisite Skills

As you look through this manual, you will see that we start our program with instruction in phoneme awareness, teaching children to segment spoken words into phonemes. You will not find activities to develop word and syllable segmentation, although we encourage you to introduce these concepts before beginning the program. Recognition of word boundaries (e.g., being able to clap out the words in a simple sentence) and the ability to segment words into syllables (e.g., being able to clap out the number of syllables in a word, such as *ham-*

burg-er) demonstrate insights about the structure of language. It is important to point out, however, that the research suggests that the most critical insight related directly to reading success is the awareness that spoken words can be segmented into phonemes, the unit of speech more or less represented by the letters of the alphabet. Thus, while we think some attention to word and syllable segmentation activities is beneficial, we focus our attention on **phoneme awareness** and include activities to develop this awareness in every lesson.

One phoneme awareness activity—*Say-It-and-Move-It*—is used each day. There is an important prerequisite for this task. The prerequisite is one-to-one correspondence—understanding that one clap (or one disk, tile, or block) stands for one sound. There are many ways of finding out whether children understand one-to-one correspondence. We have used a simple sound counting activity as follows:

Sit at a table and face the child. Give the child three disks to move from the top half of an 8 1/2" x 11" card to a heavy black horizontal line at the bottom of the card. Tell the child that you are going to knock under the table one, two, or three times. Explain that when you are finished, the child should move the number of disks that represents the number of knocks. Next, model the activity so the child knows what is expected. Finally, give the child 9 or 10 opportunities to demonstrate knowledge of one-to-one correspondence. We have found that when a child is able to move the correct number of disks three times in a row, this is a good indication that the child has grasped the concept of one-to-one correspondence. If after 10 opportunities a child has not had three successes in a row, one can conclude that the child does not yet understand one-to-one correspondence. In our research studies, we did not

Introduction

include children who could not demonstrate one-to-one correspondence on the tapping task just described. We have been told by many teachers, however, that the *Say-It-and-Move-It* activity actually helps to develop one-to-one correspondence. Consequently, we don't think there should be a hard and fast rule about whether to include in these activities children who initially lack one-to-one correspondence. This decision must be made about each child on an individual basis.

Getting Started

To help you get started, there are a few important things we would like to highlight:

1. Before beginning this program, we hope you will familiarize yourself with all of the sections of the manual. In the individual lessons, we often refer you to a previous lesson for directions, or we may refer you to the Materials Section. It will be easier to find what you need if you have spent time reviewing the entire manual. We have not chosen to tab the individual lessons, but some of you may find it helpful to do so. This may save time when you are planning your lessons.

2. You will note that each lesson has three parts. We always begin with *Say-It-and-Move-It*, our phoneme segmentation activity. This is followed by an activity to teach one of the eight letter names and letter sounds that are introduced in this program. Each lesson ends with an activity to reinforce phonological awareness. The lessons take between 15 and 20 minutes. If on a particular day you need to shorten the lesson, you may want to eliminate or shorten one of the games. We encourage you to include the *Say-It-and-Move-It* activity in every lesson, as it is the core activity in this program for developing phonological awareness.

3. On the left-hand side of each lesson, you will see Teacher Notes. Make sure that you read the Teacher Notes carefully before you introduce the lesson to your children. The notes provide directions and clarification of important points, as well as suggestions regarding pacing, individualization, and assessment. When there are no notes for a particular section, we have left lots of space for you to make notes to yourself about how the lesson went.

4. In addition to reading the Teacher Notes before introducing a lesson to your children, you will need to prepare some materials. Ideally, you should decide how many lessons you are going to do in a given week, see what you need to prepare for all of those lessons, and get the materials ready in advance. In each lesson, we tell you exactly what you need. You will find some, but not all, of the materials for each lesson in the Materials Section at the back of the manual. Even when we provide the materials (e.g., Sound Bingo cards), you will have to plan in advance to photocopy enough for your group. It will make the materials more durable if you laminate them, put them in plastic sleeves, or paste them on poster board.

    Preparation will also include gathering some materials that we do not provide. In each of the 44 lessons you will need individual disks, tiles, blocks, or buttons for each child for the phoneme segmentation activity, *Say-It-and-Move-It*. In later lessons you will need, for example, a puppet with a moveable mouth for our sound blending activity (Fix-It), a fishing pole (a dowel with a string and magnet attached) for the Let's Fish! game, and paper lunch bags for Post Office. At the beginning of the Materials Section, there is a complete list of supplies you will need for this program.

Introduction

5. To introduce the letters, we have provided a set of 8 1/2″ x 11″ alphabet picture cards that can be colored. Each picture includes the letter and objects that start with that letter sound. For example, the picture to reinforce the sound of m is a picture of "Mike the marvelous monkey." In the Materials Section, you will find a list of the jingles that describe each picture.

There are a variety of ways that you can use these pictures. For example, you can color one set, laminate it, and display each letter as it is introduced. These alphabet picture cards could remain on display so that the children can refer to them to help remember each letter sound.

Although we are providing a complete set of alphabet picture cards and phrases, we have chosen to introduce only eight letters (a, m, t, i, s, r, b, f) during this program. This does not mean, however, that we think these are the only letter names and sounds that children need to learn. The eight letters we have chosen include two short vowels and six consonants. It is possible to make a considerable number of phonetically regular consonant-vowel-consonant words using these letters. Knowledge of these sounds will be particularly useful when children start to read words at the end of this program.

6. In this program we only use short vowel sounds. The key words identified below are helpful in remembering the short vowel sounds:

    <u>a</u> as in apple, animal
    <u>i</u> as in igloo, itch
    <u>o</u> as in octopus, olive
    <u>u</u> as in umbrella, ugly
    <u>e</u> as in edge, Ed

7. Throughout this manual, you will see individual letters set off by slanted lines (e.g., /s/). When you see these slanted lines / /, they indicate that you should use the letter sound, not the letter name. When we are referring to the letter name, the letter will be underlined (e.g., <u>s</u>).

8. When you see sentences or phrases in **bold** in the individual lessons, the **bold print** indicates suggested dialogue to use with your students.

Lessons

Teacher Notes for Lesson 1

Say-It-and-Move-It

Say-It-and-Move-It is an activity designed to heighten an awareness of the phonemes in spoken words. It is intended to take approximately 5–7 minutes of each lesson and can be conducted with a group or with individual children. Children are taught to segment words by first repeating a target word and then moving one disk (or other small object, e.g., tile, block, button) for each sound that they say in the word. Finally, after the word is segmented, it is blended (spoken normally).

Say-It-and-Move-It sheets are used in each lesson. These are in the **Materials Section** of the manual and should be photocopied. (The words **Materials Section** are in bold to alert you that the materials you need to prepare [e.g., photocopy, color, cut] for the specific activity being described are provided in the manual.) For variety, you can use sheets with different pictures or shapes on different days. For the first few lessons, you might give each child a *Say-It-and-Move-It* sheet with a clown face on it. The following week, you might want to use a different *Say-It-and-Move-It* sheet for each lesson. The picture or shape is simply a place for the children to store their disks.

Proper pacing is crucial!

You should begin by modeling the correct way to segment the target word. (It is easier to model this task if your *Say-It-and-Move-It* sheet is facing the children.) First the target word is spoken; then each sound is spoken in an elongated fashion as a disk is moved for each sound. Pause only if there is a ^ sign to represent a pause. Stop sounds (sounds that cannot be held without distortion, e.g., /b/, /d/, /p/, /t/) are spoken quickly and are not elongated.

All vowels used in these activities have their short sounds. If you are unfamiliar with the short vowel sounds, you might use these key words to help you remember them:

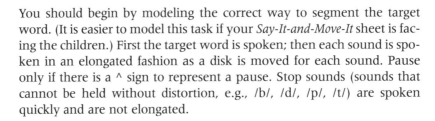

a   as in apple, animal
i   as in igloo, itch
o   as in octopus, olive
u   as in umbrella, ugly
e   as in edge, Ed

Because the *Say-It-and-Move-It* activity utilizes a lot of stimulating materials (e.g., blocks, disks, pictures), it is important to teach your students

LESSON 1

Say-It-and-Move-It

Materials: 1 *Say-It-and-Move-It* sheet per child
               2 disks or tiles per child

Review **TEACHER NOTES** for this lesson before proceeding.

Today you will work on single sounds and single sounds repeated:

/a/
/s/
/t/
/t/ ˆ /t/
(ˆ indicates a slight pause)

To begin the lesson, each child has one *Say-It-and-Move-It* sheet and one disk. You should also have a *Say-It-and-Move-It* sheet facing the children, so it is actually upside down for you.

For this first lesson, when you give directions or ask questions, it is expected that the children will respond as a group.

Teacher (T) says:
    We are going to play a game called *Say-It-and-Move-It*. What's the name of the game?
    Wait for the students to respond with *"Say-It-and-Move-It."*

T: **Watch me and listen. I'm going to say a sound. /a/.**
    Remember to use the short sound of <u>a</u> as in *apple.*

T: **Now I'm going to say it and move it.**
    Demonstrate for the children by placing your finger on a

3

Teacher Notes for Lesson 1

specific behaviors to use during the segmentation part of each lesson. If you follow these suggestions, the *Say-It-and-Move-It* activity will be more successful.

First, the children need to be sitting still on their chairs and watching you model the activity. This is an activity that requires focused attention. Remember, however, that this portion of the lesson takes only 5–7 minutes, so the expectation for focused attention is developmentally appropriate for most kindergarten children.

Next, it should be stressed to the children that only one finger of one hand should be used for moving the manipulative objects (e.g., disks, tiles, blocks). It is helpful to encourage the students to have their "moving finger" ready. You might want to have the children hold up their index (pointing) finger to show that it's ready. Some teachers sing a song or play a little game ("show me your ready finger") to encourage the children to use just one finger. If the children use two or more fingers or both hands to move the disks, it is helpful for you to say, "Watch me. I'm using only one hand and one finger of that hand. Now, you try it."

In addition, the children should always store the manipulative objects on the picture portion of their *Say-It-and-Move-It* sheets. You can be creative in your instructions depending on the particular picture you are using. For example, if the clown face is being used, you might say, "Let's give our clowns earrings or teeth with our disks today." This type of instruction may reduce the amount of fiddling or excess playing with the objects as the lesson begins. Finally, teach the children to "sweep" the objects back to the picture after completing each segmenting task.

It is important to remember that this is a listening (oral language) and sound counting activity. It is not a letter recognition activity or an activity in which the letters must be associated with sounds. Therefore, any sounds could actually be used. Because the children will learn the short sounds of the vowels during the letter sound portion of this program, we have chosen to include only short vowel sounds during the *Say-It-and-Move-It* activities in this manual. **Remember, when you see a letter inside these slanted lines / /, use the letter sound. When the letter is underlined, use the letter name.**

You will also see sentences or phrases in **bold.** This is suggested dialogue to use with your children. The script that is *not* in bold is not meant to be read aloud.

disk, drawing out (holding) the /aaa/ sound, and simultaneously moving the disk below the thick black line to the black
dot at the left hand side of the arrow at the bottom of the
Say-It-and-Move-It sheet. Then point to the disk and say,

T: **/a/, one sound.**

T: **Now I'm going to sweep the disk back to the _____
    (clown, boat, or whatever object is pictured).**
    Move the disk back to the pictured object.

T: **Now it's your turn. Listen first.**

T: **Say /a/.**

T: **What sound?**
    Wait for a response from the children.

T: **Now, say it and move it.**
    If the children have difficulty, this is a good time for you to
    model the correct response again. Say, **Watch me,** and then
    demonstrate *Say-It-and-Move-It,* just as you did earlier. The
    children should then repeat the activity with /a/, as
    described above.

T: **Let's try some different sounds.**
    Use the same procedure as above for introducing /s/ and
    /t/. *Hiss* with the /s/, and be careful with the /t/. Don't
    elongate the /t/ when you say it and move it. Say it quickly.
    Sometimes it is helpful to refer to these stop sounds as "hot
    sounds" so that the children "get off" of these sounds quickly.

T: **Now we're going to try something even harder.**
    Take a second disk.

Teacher Notes for Lesson 1

T: **Are you ready? Listen and watch me.**
I'm going to say a sound, but I may say it more than once.

T: **/t/ ^ /t/**

T: **Now I'm going to say it and move it.**
/t/ ^ /t/.
Move one disk below the line as you quickly say the first /t/, and move the second disk as you say the second /t/.

Move your finger from left to right under the two disks and say,

T: **Two sounds.**
Sweep the disks back to the picture.

Give each child a second disk.

T: **Now I want you to try it.**

T: **Ready? Listen.**
Say, /t/ ^ /t/.
Wait for the children to respond.

T: **Now, say it and move it.**
Again, wait for the children to respond and then say,

T: **How many sounds?**
If the children don't respond correctly, you should say,
Two sounds.

Have the group or individual children try various combinations of /a/, /t/, and /s/, presented as single sounds or sounds repeated.

Teacher Notes for Lesson 1

Letter Name and Sound Instruction

Like the *Say-It-and-Move-It* component of this program, *Letter Name and Sound Instruction* is a part of each lesson. It has been determined that instruction in phoneme awareness is more effective when it is combined with instruction in letter sound correspondences. If this is the first time that you are working on letter names and sounds with your children, it will help the children if you explain that **all letters have both a name and a sound.** This is an abstract concept, and many children don't understand this idea until it has been presented many times and with many examples.

Throughout the program we will be introducing several games to provide students with additional practice opportunities for mastery of letter sound correspondences. This component of the lesson will vary in length, depending on whether a game is introduced. In general, you will spend about 5–10 minutes on this portion of the lesson.

In this manual, we have chosen to introduce only eight letters. This does not mean that we think these are the only letter sounds the children need to learn. The eight sounds we have chosen include two short vowels and six consonants. Numerous phonetically regular consonant-vowel-consonant words can be made using these letters. Thus, knowledge of these sounds will be particularly useful when children start to read words at the end of this program.

Letter Name and Sound Instruction

Introducing the Letter a

Materials: Large alphabet picture card of a

Introduce the large alphabet picture card of the letter a (both large and small alphabet picture cards are in the **Materials Section** of the manual). It will add interest if you have colored this card before you show it to the children. If you do color the card, make sure that you retain a black and white copy of the picture card that can be photocopied for the children to color in later lessons.

You might tell the children that **one sound that this letter makes is /a/ (as in *apple, ant,* and *ask*)**. Talk about what you see in the alphabet picture card. Point to various parts of the picture and isolate the /a/ sound in *ant* and *apple* (e.g., **"Apple, do you hear the /a/ in *apple*?"**). Help the children think of other words that start with the /a/ sound.

Take turns asking children the letter's name. Take turns asking children the letter's sound. Then mix the two (letter name and sound).

Teacher Notes for Lesson 1

Phonological Awareness Practice

The activities suggested in this component of each lesson provide practice in a range of simple phonological awareness tasks.

Sound Categorization by Rhyme

The first activity to be introduced is Sound Categorization by Rhyme (adapted from Bradley & Bryant, 1983). That is, the children are going to practice grouping together words that rhyme. The same materials and the game description that appear in Lesson 1 will be used later in the program for Sound Categorization by Initial Sound.

To play the game, there are some things you need to prepare ahead of time. You might want to photocopy and laminate the Sound Categorization by Rhyme and Initial Sound cards from the **Materials Section** in this manual. Each page can be cut into four separate picture cards, grouped into the recommended sets, and filed by set in a recipe box. Index tabs can be used to identify each set and to separate the rhyming sets from the sets based on initial sounds. The list of recommended sets can be found on each page of cards. We have included duplicates of some pictures because some of the picture cards will be used for grouping words by rhyme and by initial sound.

You will notice in this lesson and throughout the manual that the words **Teacher Notes** are in bold. This is to draw your attention to the special instructions included in these notes.

Phonological Awareness Practice

Sound Categorization by Rhyme

Materials: 3–5 sets of Sound Categorization by Rhyme cards
Recipe box (optional, see **Teacher Notes**)
Index tabs (optional, see **Teacher Notes**)

To Play: Select a set of Sound Categorization by Rhyme cards. The players must determine which one of four pictures does not belong in a set. Place the four pictures on the table in front of the children while singing or saying the following verse:

> **One of these things is not like the others.**
> **One of these things does not belong.**
> **One of these things is not like the others.**
> **Which of these things does not belong?**

After the cards have been placed on the table and the song has been sung, ask the children to name each picture. You may need to name the pictures along with the children. Then ask the question, **"Which one does not belong?"**

Have the children tell which card doesn't belong and have them tell why (or supply the rule). For example, if the objects pictured were *hat, cat, fish,* and *bat,* the children might say, *"Hat, cat,* and *bat* all rhyme or end the same, but *fish* doesn't."*

In developing categorization by rhyme, the children may attempt to classify by some other principle, for example, by color or semantic category (e.g., farm animals). Acknowledge the correctness of their observations, and continue with a statement such as, **"Yes, that's right, but I'm thinking of a different rule. Can you think of my rule?"**

Teacher Notes for Lesson 2

Say-It-and-Move-It

Begin the *Say-It-and-Move-It* activity by modeling the first item for the children. You do not need to continue modeling if the children are able to segment correctly.

It is important to give positive feedback to the children as they segment each item. If a child has difficulty segmenting or has made an error, rather than commenting on the specific error, have all the children sweep their disks back to the picture. Then model again as follows:

T: **Watch me.**

T: **I'm going to say /t/ ^ /t/.**

T: **Now I'm going to say it and move it.**

Model, moving disks correctly.

T: **Now it's your turn.**

T: **Everybody say /t/ ^ /t/.**

T: **Now everybody say it and move it.**

One way to check whether children are able to segment independently is to give them individual turns to say it and move it.

Refer to Lesson 1 for complete directions.

LESSON 2

Say-It-and-Move-It

Materials: 1 *Say-It-and-Move-It* sheet per child
2 disks or tiles per child

Today you will use the same procedure and script that you used for Lesson 1. Give each child a *Say-It-and-Move-It* sheet and two disks. Remind the children about the *Say-It-and-Move-It* game you played in the previous lesson. Then model the activity for them.

T: **Watch me and listen. I'm going to say a sound. /a/.**

T: **Now I'm going to say it and move it.**
Place your fingers on the disk and draw out (hold) the /aaa/ sound while simultaneously moving the disk below the thick black line to the black dot at the left hand side of the arrow at the bottom of the sheet. Then point to the disk and say,

T: **/a/, one sound.**
Sweep the disk back to the pictured object.

T: **Now it's your turn. Listen first. /a/. What sound?**
Wait for a response.

T: **Now, say it and move it.**

Continue as before, using the following sounds and repeated sounds suggested for this lesson:

/a/	/i/
/a/ ^ /a/	/k/ ^ /k/
/t/ ^ /t/	/t/

Teacher Notes for Lesson 2

Letter Name and Sound Instruction

Hand-Clapping Game for <u>a</u>

When the children are successful with the simple Hand-Clapping Game described in Lesson 2 on the next page, you might want to try a more complex version of the Hand-Clapping Game described below. It is done with partners and works best when the partners face each other.

<u>**a**</u>	clap hands on thighs
<u>**a**</u>	clap hands together
What	right hands of partners clap together high
be	clap hands together
gins	left hands of partners clap together high
with	clap hands together
<u>**a**</u>?	clap hands on thighs
Ask	clap hands together
an	right hands of partners clap together high
ant	clap hands together
and	left hands of partners clap together high
an	clap hands together
ap	clap hands on thighs
ple.	clap hands together
What	right hands of partners clap together high
be	clap hands together
gins	left hands of partners clap together high
with	clap hands together
<u>**a**</u>?	clap hands on thigh

Letter Name and Sound Instruction

Hand-Clapping Game for a

Materials: Large alphabet picture card of a

Using the large alphabet picture card of the letter a, review the name and sound of a. Remember, we are using only short vowel sounds, as in *apple*. Here is a jingle you can teach the children to help them remember the sound for a:

> a   a
> What begins with a?
> Ask an ant and an apple.
> What begins with a?

The children might enjoy using the jingle with a Hand-Clapping Game. The game is as follows, with a clap on every syllable:

a	clap hands on thighs
a	clap hands together
What	clap hands on thighs
be	clap hands together
gins	clap hands on thighs
with	clap hands together
a?	clap hands on thighs
Ask	clap hands together
an	clap hands on thighs
ant	clap hands together
and	clap hands on thighs
an	clap hands together
ap	clap hands on thighs
ple.	clap hands together
What	clap hands on thighs
be	clap hands together
gins	clap hands on thighs
with	clap hands together
a?	clap hands on thighs

15

Teacher Notes for Lesson 2

Phonological Awareness Practice

We will not always have special instructions to include in **Teacher Notes.** We hope you will use these blank pages to write your own notes about the lessons.

Phonological Awareness Practice

Fix-It

Materials: Puppet with mouth that opens and closes

For this activity you will need a puppet, preferably one with a mouth that can open and close.

Explain to the children that the puppet has a funny way of talking which makes it feel shy. However, the puppet is trying to learn how to talk like boys and girls, so the children need to help fix the puppet's words.

Move the puppet's mouth while saying one of the words listed below in a drawn-out fashion (e.g., **"iiit"**). The puppet is embarrassed and turns away from the children. To help the puppet, the children say the word correctly (they blend the sounds and say the word normally). Repeat using at least five of the words listed below:

at	as
it	if
up	us
in	is
an	Ed
am	Al

Teacher Notes for Lesson 3

Say-It-and-Move-It

Remember, we are using the short vowel sounds. Use the key words to help you remember these sounds.

<u>a</u> as in apple, animal
<u>i</u> as in igloo, itch
<u>o</u> as in octopus, olive
<u>u</u> as in umbrella, ugly
<u>e</u> as in edge, Ed

Letter Name and Sound Instruction

Alphabet Books

You will need to photocopy the large alphabet picture card of the letter <u>a</u>. Alphabet picture cards are in the **Materials Section** of the manual. Make enough copies so that each child will have one to color. The children should place their colored alphabet pictures in their own alphabet book that is kept at school. If the children want to take their colored alphabet pictures home, make a second copy of the alphabet picture card to color.

LESSON 3

Say-It-and-Move-It

Materials: 1 *Say-It-and-Move-It* sheet per child
2 disks or tiles per child

Use the same procedure and script that you used in Lesson 1, and model the first item for the children. Give each child a *Say-It-and-Move-It* sheet and two disks. The following sounds and repeated sounds are to be used for this lesson:

/o/
/s/
/i/ ^ /i/
/a/
/p/ ^ /p/
/t/

Letter Name and Sound Instruction

Alphabet Books

Materials: 1 large alphabet picture card per child of <u>a</u>
Crayons

Today the children will color their own large alphabet picture cards of the letter <u>a</u>. As they are coloring, ask the children about their alphabet pictures (e.g., letter name, letter sound, and picture associations).

Teacher Notes for Lesson 3

Phonological Awareness Practice

Phonological Awareness Practice

Sound Categorization by Rhyme

Materials: 3–5 sets of Sound Categorization by Rhyme cards

Continue to work on rhyming as described in Lesson 1.

Teacher Notes for Lesson 4

Proper pacing is crucial!

Say-It-and-Move-It

Today you will be introducing the children to segmentation of real words made up of two phonemes. Although some children will be more ready for this new step than others, we want you to introduce the skill to all of the children today.

In the next few lessons, we will give you some examples of how to individualize your lessons to accommodate children who still need more practice representing one sound and one sound repeated.

We have been very selective about the two-phoneme words we have elected to use. We didn't use *of* and *add,* for example, even though both have two phonemes. The sound of o̱ in *of* is not **phonetically regular**. If the word *of* were phonetically regular, the o̱ would have the sound that one hears at the beginning of *octopus.* In this program, we use only phonetically regular words. We didn't use words like *add* because, even though *add* has two phonemes, the conventional spelling has three letters. Although the children will not be exposed to the spelling of the words we use in our *Say-It-and-Move-It* activities, we decided to maintain consistency by using only words in our oral language activities that have the same number of sounds and letters.

It is important to note that after you segment a *real word,* the children should blend the word and say it normally. Instead of saying "one sound" or "two sounds," as you did when segmenting single or repeated sounds, the final response will be to say the word normally.

To keep interest high, begin to vary the materials in this activity. You can use different *Say-It-and-Move-It* sheets (see **Materials Section**) and manipulatives, such as small colored blocks, small ceramic tiles, and buttons. You can also create your own *Say-It-and-Move-It* sheets using seasonal and holiday pictures.

LESSON 4

Say-It-and-Move-It

Materials: 1 *Say-It-and-Move-It* sheet per child
2 disks or tiles per child

We have returned to the script format to make sure the procedure for the new skill is clear. Give each child a *Say-It-and-Move-It* sheet and two disks. The first two items are a review and probably don't need to be modeled for the children.

T: **Say /a/.**

T: **Now say it and move it.**

T: **Say /a/ ^ /a/.**

T: **Now say it and move it.**

T: **Now we're going to do something different. I'm going to do it first. Listen and watch me.**

T: **I'm going to say the word *at*. *At*. Now I'm going to say it and move it.**

T: **/aaaaa/.** As you are saying /aaa/, simultaneously move one disk down to the line nearer to the ball end.
/t/. Quickly move the second disk to the line, to the immediate right of the first disk.
***At*.** This time say the word normally, moving your finger from left to right under the two disks.

T: **Now it's your turn.**

T: **Say *at*.**

23

Teacher Notes for Lesson 4

Letter Name and Sound Instruction

Introducing the Letter m

In preparation for introducing the letter m, you might want to color your copy of the large alphabet picture card.

We have suggested several adjectives to describe Mike. We use the words *moody* and *mad* to describe Mike in the Hand-Clapping Game in Lesson 6. The jingle sheet in the **Materials Section** of the manual refers to Mike as the marvelous monkey.

T: **Now say it and move it.**

T: **Say *up*.**

T: **Now say it and move it.**
If the children have difficulty segmenting *up*, model as with *at*. Be sure to elongate /uuuuu/, and say /p/ quickly. Say *up* at the end in a normal fashion. After modeling, have the children do *up* alone.

T: **Say *it*.**

T: **Now say it and move it.**

T: **Say /i/.**

T: **Now say it and move it.**

Letter Name and Sound Instruction

Introducing the Letter m

Materials: Large alphabet picture cards of a and m

Briefly review the sound and the letter name for a.

Introduce the new letter m using your colored alphabet picture card. This picture shows Mike the (decide what you want to call him—moody, mad, marvelous, magic) monkey. Exclaim for the children, ***"Hey, Mike, you look (marvelous)!"*** Tell the children that the picture will help them to remember the sound that m makes. When the children say the sound /m/, have them rub their stomachs in a circular motion (as in **"mmm mmmm good"**). Take turns asking children the letter's name. Take turns

Teacher Notes for Lesson 4

Phonological Awareness Practice

How Many Sounds?

To play How Many Sounds? the teacher pronounces a single phoneme or a two-phoneme word, holding up one finger for each sound as it is pronounced. The teacher then asks individuals or the whole group to repeat the procedure. Have students answer the question, "How many sounds?"

This activity can be extended by touching one of the upheld fingers and asking a student to pronounce the sound represented by that finger. Be careful to pronounce the words slowly, stretching the sounds but not pausing between them. Avoid words that have stop consonants in the initial position.

asking children the letter's sound. Mix the two (letter name and sound), using the colored large alphabet picture card of the letter <u>m</u>. Then use both <u>m</u> and <u>a</u> and ask children the letter name and sound of both letters.

Phonological Awareness Practice

How Many Sounds?

Materials: None

This is a game in which children match sounds in a given word to finger cues. See the **Teacher Notes** for a complete description. Use any five of the words below, mixing two-phoneme items with stop consonants at the end and two-phoneme items with continuous sounds at the end.

two-phoneme words with stop consonants at the end	two-phoneme words with continuous sounds at the end
at	an
it	in
up	am
Ed	Al
	as
	us
	is

Teacher Notes for Lesson 5

Proper pacing is crucial!

Say-It-and-Move-It

In this program, two-phoneme items that are also meaningful words are used. Although we prefer to use meaningful words for children at this age, there are some students who will need to practice two-phoneme items for a longer period of time. For those children, the teacher will need to supplement real words with two-phoneme nonwords, such as *ab*, *ig*, and *ot*.

It is important to remember that *Say-It-and-Move-It* is about counting the sounds in spoken words. It is an oral language activity and does not require that children identify the specific letters that make those sounds. Therefore, you can use words during *Say-It-and-Move-It* that include letter sounds that are *not* being taught during the letter sound portion of these lessons. For example, even though children are not expected at this point to be able to tell you which two letters are in *up*, they should be able to tell you (and show you by moving disks to represent each sound) that *up* has two sounds.

Letter Name and Sound Instruction

LESSON 5

Say-It-and-Move-It

Materials: 1 *Say-It-and-Move-It* sheet per child
2 disks or tiles per child

Continue to use the same procedure and script that were used for Lesson 1.

Following is the list of sounds and words to be used in this lesson:

/i/
/i/ ^ /i/
it
at
/u/
/u/ ^ /u/
up

Letter Name and Sound Instruction

Tracing in the Air

Materials: None

T: **Today we are going to pretend that our pointing fingers are magic pencils. We are going to use them to trace some letters in the air on our magic slates.**

Teacher Notes for Lesson 5

Alphabet Books

You will need to photocopy the large alphabet picture card of the letter m. Make enough copies so that each child will have one to color. Make a second copy if the children want to take their pictures home.

T: **The first letter we are going to trace says /m/.**

T: **Watch me.**
Stand with your back to the group so the children see the letter being formed from left to right. Use whole arm movements when making the letters with your index finger extended.

T: **Now I'll watch you trace the letter that says /m/. Everyone put your magic finger pencil in the air. Be sure to use your whole arm to help you make the letter that says /m/.**

T: **Erase your magic slates. Let's get ready to trace another letter in the air. This time we will be tracing the letter that says /a/. First watch me, and then, after I'm done, I will watch you.**
Follow the procedure you used for m.

Alphabet Books

Materials: Alphabet books
1 large alphabet picture card per child of m
Crayons

Today the children will color their own m alphabet picture. Give the children their alphabet books, and review the a alphabet picture first. Then pass out an m alphabet picture to each child to be colored. As they are coloring, ask the children about their pictures (letter name, letter sound, and picture associations).

Teacher Notes for Lesson 5

Phonological Awareness Practice

Phonological Awareness Practice

Fix-It

Materials: Puppet with mouth that opens and closes

Continue to use the puppet as described in Lesson 2. Use at least five of the following words:

at	as
it	if
up	us
in	is
an	Ed
am	Al

Teacher Notes for Lesson 6

Proper pacing is crucial!

Say-It-and-Move-It

If the children are having difficulty segmenting two-phoneme words, you may need to do more lessons using just single sounds and sounds repeated. Most children will not have difficulty at this stage, but some children may need more practice.

Here is an example of a lesson to use when one child in the group (in this case, Greg) needs more practice on one sound repeated, such as /i/ ^ /i/.

First, review the following with the group as a whole:

> **/i/**
> **/a/ ^ /a/**
> **/t/ ^ /t/**
> **up**

Next, give each child an individual turn, using items similar to the following:

> **Tyrone:**   **at**
> **Greg:**   **/v/ ^ /v/**
> **Maria:**   **if**
> **Paula:**   **/m/ ^ /m/**
> **Sam:**   **as**

You will notice in the above example that both Greg and Paula were given a single phoneme repeated. Although Greg is the group member primarily in need of practicing this lower level skill, it is important that Greg not feel singled out. Thus, during each of the individual turns, another group member (a different one for each turn) should also be given a single sound repeated.

LESSON 6

Say-It-and-Move-It

Materials: 1 *Say-It-and-Move-It* sheet per child
2 disks or tiles per child

Use the same procedure that you used in Lesson 5. Give the children two blocks, disks, tiles, or buttons.

/u/
/u/ ^ /u/
up
/e/
Ed
it
at

Teacher Notes for Lesson 6

Letter Name and Sound Instruction

Hand-Clapping Game for m

Here is a variation of the Hand-Clapping Game that is done with partners. It works best when the partners face each other.

Mike	clap hands on thighs
is	clap hands together
moo	right hands of partners clap together high
dy	clap hands together
and	left hands of partners clap together high
he's	clap hands together
mad.	clap hands on thighs
What	clap hands together
else	right hands of partners clap together high
be	clap hands together
gins	left hands of partners clap together high
with	clap hands together
m?	clap hands on thighs

Letter Name and Sound Instruction

Hand-Clapping Game for m

Materials: Large alphabet picture cards of a and m

Have your a and m alphabet picture cards out on the table. Review with the children the Hand-Clapping Game for a that was taught in Lesson 2.

Today the children will learn a Hand-Clapping Game for m.

This is the jingle: Mike is moody
and he's mad.
What else
begins with m?

Encourage the children to think of other words that start with /m/.

The game is as follows, with a clap on every syllable:

Mike	clap hands on thighs
is	clap hands together
moo	clap hands on thighs
dy	clap hands together
and	clap hands on thighs
he's	clap hands together
mad.	clap hands on thighs
What	clap hands together
else	clap hands on thighs
be	clap hands together
gins	clap hands on thighs
with	clap hands together
m?	clap hands on thighs

Teacher Notes for Lesson 6

Phonological Awareness Practice

Phonological Awareness Practice

Sound Categorization by Rhyme

Materials: 3–5 sets of Sound Categorization by Rhyme cards

Continue to work on rhyming as described in Lesson 1, using three to five sets of rhyming pictures. Remember that you might need to name the pictures in each rhyming set along with the children.

Once the children have selected the card that doesn't belong in a particular set, have them tell why it doesn't belong. For example, if the objects pictured were *hat, cat, fish,* and *bat,* the children might say, *"Hat, cat,* and *bat* all rhyme or end the same, but *fish* doesn't." Some children may attempt to classify by some other principle, for example, by color or semantic category (e.g., farm animals). Acknowledge the correctness of their observations, and continue with a statement such as, **"Yes, that's right, but I'm thinking of a different rule. Can you think of my rule?"**

Teacher Notes for Lesson 7

Say-It-and-Move-It

It is important to remember that *Say-It-and-Move-It* is about segmenting the sounds in words. It is not about matching letters to sounds (until you get to Lesson 20 and make one letter tile available). Therefore, you can use words in this part of the lesson that include sounds that are *not* being taught during the *Letter Name and Sound Instruction* portion of the lesson. For example, even though we don't expect the children at this point to be able to tell you which two letters are used to write *up*, they should be able to tell you (and show you by moving disks to represent each sound) that *up* has two sounds.

We have begun using continuous sounds in the final position in this lesson (e.g., *us*). It may be more difficult for some children to segment these words because there is not a definite stop sound at the end.

Letter Name and Sound Instruction

Sound Bingo

There are two versions of Sound Bingo. The first version, Option I, is described in the lesson. The second version, Option II, is described on page 42. To play either version of Sound Bingo, you must first make copies of each of the five Sound Bingo cards that reinforce a̲ and m̲. These cards can be found in the **Materials Section** of the manual. Each of the five large cards can be given to a different child. The cards can be laminated or placed in a plastic sheet protector to make them more durable.

Option I
See lesson for instructions.

LESSON 7

Say-It-and-Move-It

Materials: 1 *Say-It-and-Move-It* sheet per child
2 disks or tiles per child

Give the children two blocks, disks, buttons, or tiles to use in this lesson as you segment the following items:

up
Al
/a/
us
/b/ ^ /b/
in
/o/
as

Letter Name and Sound Instruction

Sound Bingo

Materials: 1 Sound Bingo card per child that reinforces <u>a</u> and <u>m</u>
Copies of students' Sound Bingo cards, cut up and
put in a box
1 handful of Bingo chips per child
1 die with letters on each side (for Option II,
see **Teacher Notes**)

Teacher Notes for Lesson 7

Option II

Prepare a die using a colored 1-inch cube. Write the letter <u>a</u> on three sides and the letter <u>m</u> on the other three sides. You can put sticky tabs or masking tape on the faces of the cube before writing the letters.

Distribute one large Sound Bingo card and a handful of chips to each child. The children roll the die in turn. After each roll, the child gives the sound of the letter he or she has rolled. The child may place a Bingo chip either on a picture that starts with the sound of the letter that is face up on the die (e.g., if an <u>m</u> is rolled, the child can place a chip on the picture of a *map*) or on the letter itself. If the child who has rolled the die chooses to cover a picture, other children who have that picture may cover theirs as well. If the child chooses to cover the letter, then other children can cover the letter. If a child has more than one <u>m</u>, however, only one can be covered. If the child who rolls the die does not have the letter that was rolled or a picture that starts with the sound of the letter that was rolled, the child says "pass" and hands the die to the next child.

Children will play Sound Bingo with letters <u>a</u> and <u>m</u>. There are two ways to play the game. Directions for Option I are included in this lesson, and directions for Option II are in the **Teacher Notes.** For both versions of the game, you will need to decide whether the children should cover one row or the entire card.

Option I

To Play: Distribute one large Sound Bingo card and a handful of Bingo chips to each child. Photocopy and cut up a second set of Sound Bingo cards into individual picture or letter squares and place them face down in a box. Draw one small square at a time and show it to the children. If a picture is drawn, the children name the picture and give the first sound. Any child who has that picture on his or her card places a Bingo chip on it. If a letter is drawn, the children give the letter sound. Any child who has that letter places a Bingo chip on the letter. If a child has more than one of the letter that is drawn, only one can be covered. If a child does not have the letter (or picture) that is drawn, that child does not cover anything.

The following objects are on the Sound Bingo cards used in this lesson:

<u>a</u> **pictures**	<u>m</u> **pictures**
ant	mailbox
apple	map
	milk
	money
	moon
	moose
	mouse

Teacher Notes for Lesson 7

Phonological Awareness Practice

Phonological Awareness Practice

How Many Sounds?

Materials: None

As described in Lesson 4, remember to raise one finger for each sound. Vary the rate of presentation. For example, if the first finger is held up alone for a second or two before raising the second finger, this will cause the children to elongate the first sound, as in /aaat/. If the fingers are raised in more rapid succession, the words would be said quickly. Choose five of the following words:

if	Ed
am	as
at	in
us	

Teacher Notes for Lesson 8

Say-It-and-Move-It

Letter Name and Sound Instruction

I'm Thinking of a Word

The I'm Thinking of a Word game may be difficult for some children. Don't give up if some of the children can't do it right away. Children who have limited vocabulary development or difficulty finding words or producing them quickly may need more "wait time" and additional clues to come up with an answer.

As the children become more proficient, they may take turns thinking of the secret word and giving the clues. When the children are taking this role, they should whisper their secret word to the teacher before giving any clues.

LESSON 8

Say-It-and-Move-It

Materials: 1 *Say-It-and-Move-It* sheet per child
2 disks or tiles per child

Use two blocks or disks, following the same procedure as in previous lessons.

/i/
is
Ed
if
/a/
us
/z/ ^ /z/

Letter Name and Sound Instruction

I'm Thinking of a Word

Materials: Large alphabet picture cards of <u>a</u> and <u>m</u>

To Play: In this game, the children guess the secret word from clues that you give them. The word should begin with one of the letters you are working on today—either <u>a</u> or <u>m</u>. To get ready to play this game, the children need a warm-up activity. Have the children think of words that start with <u>a</u> and <u>m</u>. If they have trouble, prompt them by saying, **"I'm thinking of a word that starts with /m/. We see this animal in the zoo. Yes, *monkey.*"**

Teacher Notes for Lesson 8

Phonological Awareness Practice

If the children think of a word that starts with the long <u>a</u> sound, as in *ate,* say, **"That's right, but we're looking only for words that start with the /a/ sound as in *ant, apple,* and *alligator."***

When you think the children are ready to play the game, place the alphabet picture cards for the lesson in a pile face down on the table. The first player chooses a card from the pile and shows it to all the children in the group. You ask that child to give the sound associated with the chosen letter. The child responds and places the card on the table so all can see it.

You should think of a "secret word" that begins with the sound associated with the chosen letter, and then give the children clues to guess the word. For example, if the <u>m</u> card had been chosen, you might say, **"I'm thinking of a word that begins with /m/. You wear them on your hands in winter. Yes, *mittens."*** The <u>m</u> card is then placed face down at the bottom of the pile, and the next player chooses a card from the top of the pile.

Play continues in this manner until all children have had at least one turn.

Phonological Awareness Practice

Fix-It

Materials: Puppet with mouth that opens and closes

Use the puppet and the words in the list below to play Fix-It.

Al	is
it	Ed
an	at
up	in

See Lesson 2 for directions.

Teacher Notes for Lesson 9

Say-It-and-Move-It

Letter Name and Sound Instruction

LESSON 9

Say-It-and-Move-It

Materials: 1 *Say-It-and-Move-It* sheet per child
2 disks or tiles per child

Give the children two disks or tiles, using the same procedure as in previous lessons.

/u/
/v/ ^ /v/
it
an
/e/
up
if

Letter Name and Sound Instruction

Tracing in the Air

Materials: None

Review <u>a</u> and <u>m</u> by tracing the letters in the air.

See Lesson 5 for directions.

Introducing the Letter <u>t</u>

Materials: 1 large alphabet picture card of <u>t</u>

Teacher Notes for Lesson 9

Show the children the large alphabet picture card of the letter <u>t</u>. Begin a discussion by asking them questions:

How many of you have heard the word *teenager*?
What is a teenager?
How many of you know teenagers?
What do they like to do?
One thing they like to do is talk on the telephone.
How many teenagers are in the picture?
Two talking teenagers.

Hand-Clapping Game for <u>t</u>

Materials: None

This is the jingle:

Two teens talking—
Telephone—
What else begins with <u>t</u>?

The game is as follows, with a clap on every syllable:

Two	clap hands on thighs
teens	clap hands together
talk	right hands of partners clap together high
ing–	clap hands together
Tel	left hands of partners clap together high
e	clap hands together
phone–	clap hands on thighs
What	clap hands together
else	right hands of partners clap together high
be	clap hands together
gins	left hands of partners clap together high
with	clap hands together
<u>t</u>?	clap hands on thighs

Teacher Notes for Lesson 9

Phonological Awareness Practice

Phonological Awareness Practice

How Many Sounds?

Materials: None

Use the following words:

at
am
if
as
it

See Lesson 4 for directions.

Teacher Notes for Lesson 10

Say-It-and-Move-It

LESSON 10

Say-It-and-Move-It

Materials: 1 *Say-It-and-Move-It* sheet per child
2 disks or tiles per child

Use the same procedure as in previous lessons. Use two disks, tiles, blocks, or buttons.

is
/f/
Ed
at
/i/
us

Teacher Notes for Lesson 10

Letter Name and Sound Instruction

Proper pacing is crucial!

Alphabet Books

You will need to photocopy the large alphabet picture card of the letter t. Make enough so each child will have one to color.

Periodically it is important to assess each child's mastery of the letter names and sounds taught thus far. Before introducing the letter i that is coming up in Lesson 13, you should assess each child's mastery of a, m, and t. Use the small, plain alphabet cards that don't have pictures on them (see **Materials Section**). Show the child the a card and ask for the letter name and sound. Do the same for the other two letters. Your results will be more reliable if you check each child away from the group. You might want to do this while the other children are coloring the t alphabet picture.

Based on the results of your assessment, you may decide to introduce new letters more slowly or more quickly than we have outlined in the manual. All children will not learn letter names and sounds at the same rate. As you introduce new sounds to the whole group, remember to give those children who are moving more slowly additional practice working with letter names and sounds that they have not yet mastered.

Letter Name and Sound Instruction

Hand-Clapping Game

Materials: None

Review sounds by playing Hand-Clapping Games for <u>a</u>, <u>m</u>, and <u>t</u>.

See Lessons 2, 6, or 9 for directions.

Alphabet Books

Materials: Alphabet books
          1 large alphabet picture card per child of <u>t</u>
          Crayons

Today the children will color their own large alphabet picture cards of the letter <u>t</u>. As they are coloring, ask the children about their alphabet pictures (e.g., letter name, letter sound, and picture associations).

Teacher Notes for Lesson 10

Phonological Awareness Practice

Sound Categorization by Initial Sound

The children are ready to work on categorization by initial sounds (adapted from Bradley & Bryant, 1983) when most of them have mastered rhyming. If rhyming is still difficult, continue that activity. If one or two of the children in the group are having difficulty with rhyming, you can accommodate those children by individualizing the lesson. That is, you can use sets of rhyming pictures with those children who need more practice categorizing by rhyme. Other children can use sets of pictures that start with the same initial sound.

Sets of Sound Categorization by Initial Sound cards can be found in the **Materials Section** of this manual. You will need to photocopy three to five sets for today's lesson. Cut each page into individual pictures before you begin the game. If you paste the pictures on poster board or laminate them, your materials will last longer.

Phonological Awareness Practice

Sound Categorization by Initial Sound

Materials: 3–5 sets of Sound Categorization by Initial Sound cards

Be sure to read the **Teacher Notes** about children's readiness for this activity.

To Play: Select a set of pictures that begin with the same initial sound. The players must decide which one of four pictures does not belong in the set. Place the four pictures on the table in front of the children while singing or saying the following verse:

One of these things is not like the others.
One of these things does not belong.
One of these things is not like the others.
Which of these things does not belong?

After the song has been sung and the cards have been placed on the table, ask the children to name each picture. You may need to name the pictures along with the children. Then ask the question, **"Which one does not belong?"**

Have the children tell which card doesn't belong and have them tell why (or supply the rule). For example, if the objects pictured were *cap, cot, man,* and *cup,* the children might say, *"Cap, cot,* and *cup* all start with the same sound, but *man* doesn't."

Teacher Notes for Lesson 11

Say-It-and-Move-It

Letter Name and Sound Instruction

Sound Bingo

To play either version of Sound Bingo described in Lesson 7, you must first make copies of each of the five Sound Bingo cards that reinforce the letters a, m, and t. These cards can be found in the **Materials Section** of the manual.

LESSON 11

Say-It-and-Move-It

Materials: 1 *Say-It-and-Move-It* sheet per child
2 disks or tiles per child

Use the same procedure as in previous lessons. Use two disks, tiles, or blocks.

/s/
am
up
/t/ ^ /t/
in
Al

Letter Name and Sound Instruction

Sound Bingo

Materials: 1 Sound Bingo card per child that reinforces
a, m, and t
Copies of students' Sound Bingo cards, cut up and
put in a box
1 handful of Bingo chips per child
1 die with letters on each side (for Option II)

Play using either Option I or Option II as described in Lesson 7. With Option II, the 1-inch cube will have an a on two sides, an m on two sides, and a t on two sides.

Teacher Notes for Lesson 11

Phonological Awareness Practice

You may have noticed that some lessons are a little longer than others. For example, a lesson with How Many Sounds? and I'm Thinking of a Word will be shorter because there are no manipulative materials for the children to use. Alternatively, a lesson with Sound Bingo and Sound Categorization by Rhyme and/or Initial Sound will take longer because these games have manipulative materials. Feel free to alter the activities to make a lesson longer or shorter depending on the needs of your children. For example, if you usually use five or six sets of pictures for Sound Categorization by Rhyme and/or Initial Sound, use only three if you want a shorter lesson. For Sound Bingo, you might have the children cover only one row instead of the whole card.

The following pictures are on the Sound Bingo cards:

a pictures	**m pictures**	**t pictures**
ambulance	map	telephone
ant	milk	television
apple	money	tiger
	monkey	toaster
	mouse	toe
	mummy	turtle

Phonological Awareness Practice

Sound Categorization by Initial Sound

Materials: 3–5 sets of Sound Categorization by Initial Sound cards

Continue to work on categorizing pictures by initial sound as described in Lesson 10, using three to five initial sound sets.

Teacher Notes for Lesson 12

Say-It-and-Move-It

Today we are introducing a third disk. Having more disks than are needed to segment the one- and two-phoneme items in this lesson can give you important diagnostic information about the children. Watching to see which children use the extra disk (even though it is not needed) will let you know which children are merely using whatever manipulatives are put in front of them and which children understand the concept of two-phoneme segmentation.

After you complete segmenting some items with the whole group, you might want to have the children take turns. This way, you can concentrate your attention on one child at a time and determine who is having difficulty. As the children take turns, you should model for any child who is having trouble.

LESSON 12

Say-It-and-Move-It

Materials: 1 *Say-It-and-Move-It* sheet per child
3 disks or tiles per child

Today give the children three disks, tiles, blocks, or buttons.
Begin with a dialogue such as:

T: **What is different?**

T: **Yes, we have three disks (or blocks).**

T: **Today I might trick you. You must watch me very carefully so you don't get tricked.**

T: **Watch me.**

T. *Up.*

T: **Now I'm going to say it and move it. /uuuup/.**
As you are saying this, move two disks to segment the word as usual. Point to the disks and sweep your finger underneath the disks while saying *up.*

T: **There are two sounds in *up,* so I used two disks.**

T: **How many sounds in *up?* Two. Good.**

T: **How many disks did I move? Two. Good.**

T: **I have three disks, but I only needed to use two this time.**
Sweep disks back to the picture.

Teacher Notes for Lesson 12

T: **Let's try another one.**
Use the same procedure as above, this time saying *am.*

T: **Now it's your turn. Remember, I might trick you. You must listen and think before you move your disks.**

T: **Ready?**

Use the following items for the rest of the lesson. Model a second time only if children are having trouble.

/u/
up
/a/
an
/t/ ^ /t/
at

Teacher Notes for Lesson 12

Letter Name and Sound Instruction

Letter Name and Sound Instruction

Hand-Clapping Game

Materials: None

Review sounds by playing Hand-Clapping Games for <u>a</u>, <u>m</u>, and <u>t</u>. See Lessons 2, 6, or 9 for directions.

I'm Thinking of a Word

Materials: Large alphabet picture cards of <u>a</u>, <u>m</u>, and <u>t</u>

Select words that start with the sounds of the letters <u>a</u>, <u>m</u>, and <u>t</u>. See Lesson 8 for directions.

Teacher Notes for Lesson 12

Phonological Awareness Practice

Phonological Awareness Practice

Fix-It

Materials: Puppet with mouth that opens and closes

Use the puppet as described in Lesson 2, and have the children fix at least five of the following words:

fat	sit
am	rat
is	ram
sat	at

The Fix-It activity can be extended by having the puppet read a story and say some of the words slowly, stretching them out (e.g., "faaat") and holding the sounds. The children then "fix" the words by blending them (saying them normally).

Use the story below and say the bolded, italicized words slowly.

The Adventures of Ed the Cat

There once was a cat named **Ed.**
Who was very, very **fat.**
He couldn't even **run.**
He couldn't chase the pup.
He couldn't even chase **Al,** the **rat.**
Every time **Ed** saw **Al,** his mouth watered.
He really wanted that **rat!**
Ed thought, **if** I go on a diet, I will be able to catch **Al.**
Will **Ed** go on a diet?
Will **Ed** catch and eat **Al?**

to be continued . . .

73

Teacher Notes for Lesson 13

Say-It-and-Move-It

As in Lesson 12, we will continue to give the children more disks than are actually needed for the *Say-It-and-Move-It* activity. Watch carefully to see if any of the children need extra help, now that they have an extra disk.

LESSON 13

Say-It-and-Move-It

Materials: 1 *Say-It-and-Move-It* sheet per child
3 disks or tiles per child

Give the children three disks, blocks, tiles, or buttons. Ask the children:

T: **What might have happened if you hadn't been careful yesterday? Yes, you might have been tricked.**

T: **Today I'm going to see if you remember how to move your disks carefully so you don't get tricked.**

T: **Let's try one together for review.**

T: **Say *it*. Now say it and move it.**

T: **How many sounds are there in *it*? Two. Good.**

T: **How many disks did we move? Two. Good. Let's sweep our disks back to the picture.**

T: **Now it's your turn to play. Are you ready?**

/s/
if
Al
us
Ed
as

Teacher Notes for Lesson 13

Letter Name and Sound Instruction

Letter Name and Sound Instruction

Introducing the Letter i

Materials: 1 large alphabet picture card of i

Introduce the letter i using your colored large alphabet picture card. Discuss the word *igloo.*

Teach the children the sound of /i/ as in *itch* and *igloo,* and also review the letter name. Have the children wrinkle their noses as if they were saying "ick."

Tracing in the Air

Materials: None

Review past sounds by tracing the letters a, m, and t in the air. Afterward, practice the new letter i by tracing it in the air as well.

See Lesson 5 for directions.

Teacher Notes for Lesson 13

Phonological Awareness Practice

Elkonin Cards

This activity is adapted from the work of a Russian psychologist named D.B. Elkonin (1973).

To prepare for this activity, you will need to make copies of each of the Elkonin cards found in the **Materials Section** of the manual. You will need one complete set for yourself and one complete set for every child in the group. When we used Elkonin cards in our research, we found it helpful to laminate all the cards and put them in a spiral-bound book. It is easier for the children to flip pages in a book than it is to have to collect each card after it is used and then pass out a new card. Laminating the cards will make them more durable.

Please note that in this lesson you will be using the first Elkonin card *(map)* three times. This will give the children practice with this new segmentation procedure. Be sure the children are moving the tiles into the boxes from left to right.

Phonological Awareness Practice

Elkonin Cards

Materials: Elkonin cards: map, sub, leg, nut, zip (1 per child)
3 disks or tiles per child

This activity is similar to *Say-It-and-Move-It*. Give each child three tiles and the first Elkonin card from the list below. You should also have a copy of the card placed so that it is facing the children.

For this lesson, use the following Elkonin cards:

map
sub
leg
nut
zip

Demonstrate with the tiles as the children watch.

T: **What is this picture? Yes. This is a *map*.**

T: **I'm going to put my three tiles on the picture of the *map*.**

T: **Now I'm going to say the sounds in the word *map* and move my tiles to show each sound.**

While elongating or holding the sound /mmmm/, move one of the tiles to the first box facing the children on the left. (This will be your right. We want the sounds to be placed in the boxes in order from the children's left to right.)

Teacher Notes for Lesson 13

While elongating the sound /aaaa/, move the second tile to the middle box.

Then quickly move the third tile to the last box while making the /p/ sound.

T: ***Map.***

T: **Now I'm going to say the sounds in *map* again. This time you'll move a tile each time I say a new sound.**

Name the picture again, and then say it slowly as the children move a tile for each sound you say. When all the tiles have been moved into the boxes, repeat the word in a normal fashion. Have the children move their tiles back into their pictures.

Now ask the children (or an individual child) to say the name of the picture. Have them say it again slowly, moving one tile for each sound, as before. It is important for the children to move their tiles into the boxes from left to right. You may need to show some of the children which box to use first. Finish by having the children repeat the word normally.

Give the children the next card and continue as above.

Teacher Notes for Lesson 14

Say-It-and-Move-It

This is a major transition point because it is the first time that three-phoneme words are introduced in the *Say-It-and-Move-It* activity.

If some of your children aren't consistently segmenting two-phoneme items, they should not be asked to segment words with three phonemes. As we described in Lesson 6, you can individualize the lesson by giving single sounds, single sounds repeated, and two-phoneme words to those children who need to remain at that level and giving three-phoneme words to those children who are ready for three-phoneme segmentation.

In this lesson, you will also notice that we work through a pattern to introduce the segmentation of three-phoneme words. That is, we go from /a/ to *at* to *sat*. Using a carefully sequenced pattern makes it easier to focus the children's attention on the addition of one phoneme at each step. Once children are comfortable segmenting three-phoneme words that are part of a pattern, we discontinue the pattern and present items more randomly. We want to make sure that children are using their awareness of the sounds in words and not just memorizing patterns.

Here are additional patterned lists that you can use for the next few days if your children need more practice at this level of instruction (read down):

/a/	/a/	it
am	/a/ ^ /a/	fit
ram	an	lit
Sam	man	/p/ ^ /p/
/t/ ^ /t/	van	/a/
/i/	it	at
in	lit	rat
fin	fit	fat

82

LESSON 14

Say-It-and-Move-It

Materials: 1 *Say-It-and-Move-It* sheet per child
3 disks or tiles per child

Review TEACHER NOTES for this lesson before proceeding.

Be sure to review the Teacher Notes for this lesson before you proceed. This is a major transition point.

Give the children three tiles.

T: **Today we are going to try some harder words. You must watch me very carefully.**

T: ***Sat.***

Demonstrate *Say-It-and-Move-It* with the three tiles.

T: **How many tiles did I move? Three. Good.**

T: **You must listen very carefully before you move the tiles. Some words will need one tile, some will need two tiles, and some will need all three tiles.**

T: **Ready to play? It's your turn.**

/a/
at
sat
/i/
it
sit

Teacher Notes for Lesson 14

Letter Name and Sound Instruction

Review

See the **Materials Section** of the manual for a list of the jingles that go with all of the alphabet picture cards.

Concentration

To play this simple matching game, you will need to make at least two copies of the small, plain alphabet cards (without pictures) of the letters a, m, t, and i that you will find in the **Materials Section** of the manual. To make the game more appropriate for a larger group, you might want to make four copies of each picture so that each letter has two pairs.

/a/
an
fan

If students have difficulty with the three-phoneme words, stop and model again before going on.

Letter Name and Sound Instruction

Review

Materials: List of jingles
Large alphabet picture cards of <u>a</u>, <u>m</u>, <u>t</u>, and <u>i</u>

Review the jingles for alphabet picture cards of the letters <u>a</u>, <u>m</u>, <u>t</u>, and <u>i</u> without hand clapping.

Concentration

Materials: Small, plain alphabet cards of <u>a</u>, <u>m</u>, <u>t</u>, and <u>i</u>
(multiple pairs, see **Teacher Notes**)

To Play: This is a simple matching game used to reinforce letter names and sounds. Use the <u>a</u>, <u>m</u>, <u>t</u>, and <u>i</u> small, plain alphabet cards (without pictures) and shuffle them to make sure they are in random order. Then, place the cards face down in rows on the table in front of the children. The children try to find matching pairs. The first player turns one card and then another face up, placing them down in exactly the same spot where they were when they were face down. The child names *and* gives the

Teacher Notes for Lesson 14

Phonological Awareness Practice

initial sound of the letter on each of the two cards. If the same letter is on both cards, the child keeps those cards. If the letters do not match, the player turns them face down once again in exactly the same spot, and the play passes to the next child.

The players try to remember where the cards are so that they can make matches in a later turn. After all the cards have been matched, each player reads through his or her cards, naming the letters and giving the initial sound. (To make this game more challenging, the players could also give a word that begins with the letter on each of their pairs of cards.)

Phonological Awareness Practice

Sound Categorization by Initial Sound

Materials: 3–5 sets of Sound Categorization by Initial Sound cards

Continue to work on categorizing pictures by initial sound as described in Lesson 10, using three to five sets of Sound Categorization by Initial Sound cards. Remember that you may need to name the pictures in each set along with the children.

Once the children have selected the card that doesn't belong in a particular set, have them tell why it doesn't belong. For example, if the objects pictured were *cap, cot, man,* and *cup,* the children might say, "*Cap, cot,* and *cup* all start with the same sound, but *man* doesn't."

Teacher Notes for Lesson 15

Say-It-and-Move-It

In *Say-It-and-Move-It*, you will notice that we use words that contain letters we have not yet introduced in the *Letter Name and Sound Instruction* portion of the lesson. That is because *Say-It-and-Move-It* is about recognizing the number of sounds in a word. It is not about identifying the specific letters that represent those sounds (until we get to Lesson 20 and make one letter tile available). Therefore, we can use words in this part of the lesson that include sounds which are *not* being taught during *Letter Name and Sound Instruction*. For example, even though we don't expect the children at this point to be able to tell you which two letters are in *up*, they should be able to tell you (and show you by moving disks to represent each sound) that *up* has two sounds.

LESSON 15

Say-It-and-Move-It

Materials: 1 *Say-It-and-Move-It* sheet per child
3 disks or tiles per child

Use three disks, tiles, blocks, or buttons. (It is common for the children to want to build things with their blocks now that they have more than two. If this occurs, give them a minute to build and then tell them it's time for *Say-It-and-Move-It* to begin.)

at
fat
/k/ ^ /k/
in
fin
/o/
fun

If children have any problem with the three-phoneme words, review by using the sequenced patterns described in Lesson 14.

Teacher Notes for Lesson 15

Letter Name and Sound Instruction

Alphabet Books

You will need to photocopy the large alphabet picture card of the letter i. Make enough copies so each child will have one to color.

As we mentioned earlier, periodically it is important to assess each child's mastery of the letter names and sounds taught thus far. Before introducing the letter s in Lesson 19, you should assess each child's mastery of a, m, t, and i. Use the small, plain alphabet cards that don't have pictures on them (see **Materials Section**). Show the child the a card and ask for the letter name and sound. Do the same for the other three letters. Your results will be more reliable if you check each child away from the group. You might want to do this while the other children are coloring the i alphabet picture card.

Letter Name and Sound Instruction

Alphabet Books

Materials: Alphabet books
1 large alphabet picture card per child of i
Crayons

Have the children color the i alphabet picture.

Review

Materials: List of jingles
Small, plain alphabet cards of a, m, t, and i

Using the small, plain alphabet cards, have the children identify the letter sounds and repeat the jingles for a, m, t, and i. See the **Materials Section** of the manual for a list of the jingles that go with all the alphabet picture cards.

Teacher Notes for Lesson 15

Phonological Awareness Practice

Let's Fish!

This is the first time we will be introducing the game Let's Fish! If you don't have the materials to play this game, you might want to look at the game introduced in Lesson 23, Post Office, and use a version of that game instead.

To prepare for this game, you will need to create a fishing pole by tying a string with a magnet attached to it to one end of a dowel-type stick.

The "fish" that the children will catch are pictures of objects that start with whichever sounds you are working on in a particular lesson. You can use commercially prepared pictures or pictures cut from magazines and pasted onto squares of poster board, or you can photocopy and cut up the Sound Bingo cards in the **Materials Section** of the manual, using the individual pictures as the "fish." If you use the pictures from the Sound Bingo cards, you will need to make them sturdy by laminating them or pasting them on poster board. Some teachers have pasted the pictures on poster board cut out in the shape of fish. On the back of each picture, attach a small piece of magnetic tape or put a paper clip on each picture so it can be picked up by the magnet on the fishing pole.

If you need to make the lesson shorter, either use fewer pictures for each sound or eliminate one of the sounds.

Phonological Awareness Practice

Let's Fish!

Materials: Fishing pole (see **Teacher Notes**)
5 "fish" (picture cards) representing each of the
sounds being reviewed: /a/, /m/, /t/, and /i/
(see **Teacher Notes**)

To Play: The children will isolate and identify the first sound of words that begin with /a/, /m/, /t/, and /i/. Have the children sit around the table. The "fish" (picture cards) are placed randomly in the center of the table with the picture side down. The first player extends the fishing rod and catches a fish by means of the magnet on the end of the pole. When a fish is caught, the child names the picture and gives the initial sound. For example, if the child catches a picture of a *map,* the child would respond, *"Map, /m/."* If the response is correct, the child keeps the fish. If not, the fish is placed back on the table, face down with the other picture cards. Either way, the play then passes to the next child.

Enough fish should be available to allow each child several turns. How many turns each child gets depends on the size of the group, but each child should have the same number of opportunities.

Teacher Notes for Lesson 16

Proper pacing is crucial!

Say-It-and-Move-It

Remember, as we discussed in the introduction, although some consonants can be held or elongated with little distortion (e.g., /ssssss/, /ffffff/, /mmmmmm/), the stop consonants must be said quickly in order to distort their sounds as little as possible (e.g., /t/, /p/, /b/). If you try to elongate a stop consonant, you will be adding a vowel sound, as in /buh/ or /tuh/.

It is also important to remember that to ensure a high rate of correct responses, you will have to vary the level of your questions to meet the needs of individual children. For example, when you ask the children to represent the sounds in a word with blocks, you might ask the child progressing most quickly to represent the sounds in *sun,* whereas a child progressing more slowly would be asked to represent the sounds in *it.* By individualizing in this way, each child has the opportunity to be successful.

LESSON 16

Say-It-and-Move-It

Materials: 1 *Say-It-and-Move-It* sheet per child
3 disks or tiles per child

Give the children three tiles, disks, or blocks.

am
Sam
/a/
is
met
up
lit

Teacher Notes for Lesson 16

Letter Name and Sound Instruction

Sound Bingo

To play either version of Sound Bingo as described in Lesson 7, you must first make copies of each of the five Sound Bingo cards that reinforce the letters a̲, m̲, t̲, and i̲. These cards can be found in the **Materials Section** of the manual.

Letter Name and Sound Instruction

Sound Bingo

Materials: 1 Sound Bingo card per child that reinforces <u>a</u>, <u>m</u>, <u>t</u>, and <u>i</u>

Copies of students' Sound Bingo cards, cut up and put in a box

1 handful of Bingo chips per child

1 die with letters on each side (for Option II)

Play using <u>a</u>, <u>m</u>, <u>t</u>, and <u>i</u>. You may use either Option I or II as described in Lesson 7. If you use Option II, two of the letters will be on the cube twice and two of the letters will be on the cube only once.

The following pictures are on the Sound Bingo cards:

<u>a</u> pictures	<u>m</u> pictures	<u>t</u> pictures	<u>i</u> pictures
ambulance	map	tiger	igloo
ant	milk	toaster	iguana
apple	moon	toe	insects
	moose	T-rex	
	mouse		
	mummy		

Teacher Notes for Lesson 16

Phonological Awareness Practice

Phonological Awareness Practice

Fix-It

Materials: Puppet with mouth that opens and closes

Use the puppet for this activity as described in Lesson 2. Remember, the puppet says each word in a drawn-out fashion (e.g., "maaat") and the children "fix it" by blending the sounds and saying the word normally. Choose any five of the following, and have the children fix the words.

mat	sit
zap	hut
hip	vet
lap	

Then have the puppet read Part II of **The Adventures of Ed the Cat.** Say the bolded, italicized words slowly (e.g., "naaap"), and have the children fix the words by blending the sounds.

The Adventures of Ed the Cat

That afternoon Ed took a ***nap.***
In his dreams, he was ***not fat.***
He could ***run*** fast. He could catch ***Al.***
He had on a ***red*** bib.
He ***had*** a pan on the stove.
Who was in the pan?
Was ***it*** Al?
Ed licked his lips.
Just then ***zap!***
Al woke Ed ***up*** from his ***nap.***
Ed was all ***wet.***
Al thought, "This ***is fun.***"
Ed said, "I'll get you ***yet!***"

to be continued...

Teacher Notes for Lesson 17

Say-It-and-Move-It

Remember, throughout this manual the slanted lines / / are used to indicate the letter's sound. Whenever you see a vowel inside the / /, use the short sound of the vowel. Only the short sounds are used in this program.

<u>a</u>   as in apple, animal
<u>i</u>   as in igloo, itch
<u>o</u>   as in octopus, olive
<u>u</u>   as in umbrella, ugly
<u>e</u>   as in edge, Ed

Letter Name and Sound Instruction

LESSON 17

Say-It-and-Move-It

Materials: 1 *Say-It-and-Move-It* sheet per child
3 disks or tiles per child

Give the children three disks, tiles, blocks, or buttons.

zip
/p/ ^ /p/
/e/
set
in
rag
/o/
lot

Letter Name and Sound Instruction

I'm Thinking of a Word

Materials: Large alphabet picture cards of <u>a</u>, <u>m</u>, <u>t</u>, and <u>i</u>

Play using alphabet picture cards for <u>a</u>, <u>m</u>, <u>t</u>, and <u>i</u>.

See Lesson 8 for directions.

Teacher Notes for Lesson 17

Phonological Awareness Practice

Elkonin Cards

If you introduced Elkonin cards with your children in Lesson 13, then you have already made copies of each of the Elkonin cards found in the **Materials Section** of the manual. You will need one complete set for yourself and one complete set for every child in the group.

Remember, make sure the children can identify each picture before you ask them to segment.

Phonological Awareness Practice

Elkonin Cards

Materials: Elkonin cards: mat, lip, fan, net, sun (1 per child)
3 disks or tiles per child

Give each child three tiles, and follow the same procedure as in Lesson 13 using the following pictures:

mat
lip
fan
net
sun

Teacher Notes for Lesson 18

Say-It-and-Move-It

Please note that although we are giving the children additional disks in this lesson, we are going to continue to use only three-phoneme real words. We stayed with three-phoneme words, as opposed to four- or five-phoneme words, such as *last* or *splat*, because we think that developing phonological insight with three-phoneme words is adequate at this age and developmental level. However, it may be helpful to use four- and five-phoneme words with older children who are receiving remedial instruction because it provides them with more challenging words and a deeper insight about the phonological structure of words.

Letter Name and Sound Instruction

Go Fish

To prepare for this new game, you will need to make multiple copies of the small, plain alphabet cards found in the **Materials Section** of the manual. You will need an even number of each letter because the children are trying to collect matched pairs of the alphabet cards. To play the game with four children, you might want to make eight copies of each of the four letters you are using: a, m, t, and i. If you laminate the cards or paste each card onto poster board, it will make them sturdier and the materials will last longer.

LESSON 18

Say-It-and-Move-It

Materials: 1 *Say-It-and-Move-It* sheet per child
4 disks or tiles per child

Today, give the children four disks, tiles, blocks, or buttons.

T: **What do you see that's different today? Yes, we have four tiles.**

is
sip
/u/
run
let
mop
Ed

Letter Name and Sound Instruction

Go Fish

Materials: Small, plain alphabet cards of <u>a</u>, <u>m</u>, <u>t</u>, and <u>i</u>
(multiple pairs, see **Teacher Notes**)

To Play: Shuffle the cards and deal four cards, one at a time, to each player. Place the remaining cards face down in the center of the table. Players fan their cards and hold them. (The children may need help with this step.)

Teacher Notes for Lesson 18

Phonological Awareness Practice

The first player begins by asking the child to the right for a card that will match one of those in his or her own hand. The child can ask by letter name or by letter sound. If the selected player has a matching card, the card must be given to the first player. If the selected player does not have a match, the player says, "Go fish!" The first child then draws a card from the center of the table. If the child draws the card originally requested, the card is shown to the group. The child places the card face up on top of the matching card, giving the name and sound of the letter. If the child draws an unwanted card, it is added to his or her hand. Either way, play then passes to the next player.

If a child runs out of cards by making pairs, the child draws another card from the center of the table and continues to play until all the cards are used.

At the end of the game, the players can give the name and sound of the letter on each of their pairs before handing the cards back to the teacher.

Phonological Awareness Practice

Sound Categorization by Rhyme

Materials: 3–5 sets of Sound Categorization by Rhyme cards

Continue to review categorizing by rhyme.

See Lesson 1 for directions.

Teacher Notes for Lesson 19

Say-It-and-Move-It

LESSON 19

Say-It-and-Move-It

Materials: 1 *Say-It-and-Move-It* sheet per child
4 disks or tiles per child

Give the children four disks, tiles, blocks, or buttons.

sag
is
rap
lit
Al
fed
/e/

Teacher Notes for Lesson 19

Proper pacing is crucial!

Letter Name and Sound Instruction

As we discussed before starting Lesson 1, in the 44 lessons in this manual we have chosen to introduce only eight letters. This does not mean that we think these are the only letter sounds the children need to learn. The eight sounds we have chosen include two short vowels and six consonants. It is possible to make a considerable number of phonetically regular consonant-vowel-consonant words using these letters. Thus, knowledge of these sounds will be particularly useful when children start to read words at the end of this program.

We assume that a goal in most kindergarten classes is to teach the sounds of all the letters (consonants and the short sounds of the vowels). However, because we originally used these lessons with kindergarten children who knew only two letter sounds when we began our program in the second half of the school year, we chose to introduce new letter sounds slowly. This pacing may or may not be appropriate for your children. You may want to introduce additional letter sounds more quickly. **You are the only one who can decide the most appropriate pacing for your students.**

Letter Name and Sound Instruction

Introducing the Letter s

Materials: Large alphabet picture card of s
                1 disk or tile per child

Tell the children they will "hissss" like a snake when they say /s/. Show the children the alphabet picture card for the letter s.

Practice saying, **"Six silly, slimy, slithering snakes"** to reinforce the sound of the letter s.

Discuss *slimy* and *slithering.*

Give each child a disk. Have each child say, "Six silly, slimy, slithering snakes," as he or she slides a disk to the center of the table. The children can make their disks slither like a snake as they move them.

Tracing in the Air

Materials: None

Trace the letters a, m, t, and i.

See Lesson 5 for directions.

Teacher Notes for Lesson 19

Phonological Awareness Practice

Phonological Awareness Practice

Fix-It

Materials: Puppet with mouth that opens and closes

Use the puppet for the story **The Adventures of Ed the Cat** Part III. Remind the children that the last time they heard about Ed the Cat, Al had squirted Ed in the face and had gotten him wet. Ed woke up mad.

Remember to have the puppet say the bolded, italicized words slowly, stretching them out (e.g., "maaad"). Have the children fix the words by blending the sounds and saying the words normally.

The Adventures of Ed the Cat

Ed woke up ***mad.***
Cats do not like to get ***wet.***
"I will get you, ***Al!***"
Al laughed.
"You are too ***fat*** to catch me, Ed."
Just then, Al fell on the ***wet*** floor.
Ed grabbed Al by ***his*** tail.
Al yelled, *"**Let** me go!"*
Ed held Al ***up*** by his tail.
Al could ***not*** get loose.

Ask the children to finish the story. What will happen to Al?

Teacher Notes for Lesson 20

Proper pacing is crucial!

Say-It-and-Move-It

This is a major transition point because it is the first time we are using a tile (disk, block, or button) with a letter on it. When the children can consistently segment one-, two-, and three-phoneme words correctly *and* when the children *automatically* associate the letter <u>a</u> with the short sound /a/, you can begin giving them a tile with a lowercase <u>a</u> on it.

It is important to note, however, that children should not be asked to use letter tiles unless they can automatically associate the printed letter with its sound. We want the children to concentrate on only one new task at a time. Asking the children to segment the word and move a letter tile at the same time should be done only if the association between the printed letter and the spoken sound is already automatic.

What should you do if only some of the children in your group are ready to use a letter tile? Teachers have handled this in a variety of ways. Some have delayed the introduction of letter tiles until more of the children were ready. You may have some children or an entire group who will need all blank tiles for several more weeks. Other teachers have given all children the <u>a</u> tile (or whatever tile was being used that day) but reminded the children that they didn't have to use the letter tile and that they could keep using all blank tiles for *Say-It-and-Move-It*.

Other teachers have been quite successful individualizing within the group, giving the letter tile only to those children who are ready. If you individualize in this way, the group lesson can proceed with the same examples (sounds and words) for all the children to segment. Some children will use all blank tiles, and some children will use a mix of blank tiles and letter tiles. Children who are not yet able to associate letter names and sounds may be quite happy to have only blank tiles to use during this activity, even if other children in the group are starting to use letter tiles.

You are the only one who can decide when your children are ready to use letter tiles, because you are the only one who has been watching these children on a daily basis. In Lessons 20 through 44, we suggest at the beginning of each lesson that you give each child one letter tile and the rest blanks. It will be up to you to decide if that is appropriate. **If you are not using letter tiles at all or if you are using them with only some of the children, you must alter the lesson script accord-**

114

LESSON 20

Say-It-and-Move-It

Materials: 1 *Say-It-and-Move-It* sheet per child
3 blank disks or tiles per child
1 disk or tile per child with <u>a</u>

Review TEACHER NOTES for this lesson before proceeding.

This is another major transition point. Be sure to review the Teacher Notes before you proceed.

Give the children three blank tiles and one tile with <u>a</u> on it.

T: **What is different about *Say-It-and-Move-It* today?**

T: **Yes. We have four tiles. One has the letter <u>a</u> on it.**

T: **You can use the <u>a</u> to show me where the /a/ sound would go.**

T: **Watch me.**
Demonstrate *Say-It-and-Move-It* with the word *at,* showing the children how to move the <u>a</u> tile and then a blank tile. Repeat using the word *sat.*

T: **Let's try it together. Ready?**
Repeat the procedure, moving your tiles at the same time that the children move their tiles. Use the words *at* and *sat.*

Teacher Notes for Lesson 20

ingly. Don't hesitate to use all blank tiles (give each child four) or to use a particular letter tile (and word list) over several lessons to create the most appropriate learning opportunities for your children.

To prepare for this lesson, mark the tiles (disks, blocks, or buttons) with letters. If you are using opaque material, such as blocks or ceramic tiles, you can write directly on the surface with a marking pen of contrasting color. If you are using a manipulative that has a transparent or irregular surface, such as Bingo chips, you might affix a small, self-sticking label to the surface and write the letter on the label.

Letter Name and Sound Instruction

Alphabet Books

When reviewing the sounds for <u>a</u> and <u>i</u>, you might point out to the children that when you make the /a/ sound your mouth looks like you might be about to bite an apple. When you make the /i/ sound, your mouth is opened less.

You will need to photocopy the large alphabet picture card of the letter <u>s</u>. Make enough copies so each child will have one to color. Make a second copy if the children want to take their pictures home.

While the children are coloring their <u>s</u> alphabet pictures, it might be a good time to check individually for mastery of sounds taught thus far. See the **Teacher Notes** for Lesson 10 for suggestions.

T: **You can use your <u>a</u> if you want, or you can use just the blank tiles.**

/a/
at
fat
as
sat
map
am

Letter Name and Sound Instruction

Alphabet Books

Materials: Alphabet books
1 large alphabet picture card per child of <u>s</u>
Crayons

Give the children their alphabet books, and review the letter sounds by going through the pages.

Give the children their <u>s</u> alphabet pictures to color. As they are coloring, ask the children about their pictures (letter name, letter sound, and picture associations).

Teacher Notes for Lesson 20

Phonological Awareness Practice

Sound Categorization by Rhyme and Initial Sound

If the children are having trouble categorizing pictures by either rhyme or initial sound, continue to practice one or the other and don't mix them until both skills are solid. If only some children in the group are having difficulty, you can individualize the lesson. For example, children who need more practice categorizing by rhyme can be given sets of pictures that rhyme, whereas other children can be given sets of pictures that rhyme and (during another turn) sets of pictures that can be categorized by initial sound.

Phonological Awareness Practice

Sound Categorization by Rhyme and Initial Sound

Materials: 4 sets of Sound Categorization by Rhyme cards
4 sets of Sound Categorization by Initial Sound cards

Today you will use four sets of rhyming pictures and four sets of initial sound pictures. When you play, the first set you use might be pictures that rhyme, the second set might be pictures that can be categorized by initial sound, the third set might also be pictures that can be categorized by initial sound, and the fourth set might be pictures that rhyme. You want to avoid having a predictable pattern.

See Lessons 1 and 10 for complete descriptions of categorizing by rhyme or initial sound.

Teacher Notes for Lesson 21

Say-It-and-Move-It

Before you introduce this lesson, you may want to review the **Teacher Notes** from Lesson 20 regarding the use of letter tiles. Remember, even though we suggest at the beginning of Lessons 20 through 44 that each child be given a letter tile, it is up to you to decide when it is appropriate to use letter tiles with your students. If you aren't using letter tiles or if you are using them with only some children, you will need to alter the lesson script accordingly. Each child should always have four tiles (three blank tiles and one letter tile, or four blank tiles).

LESSON 21

Say-It-and-Move-It

Materials: 1 *Say-It-and-Move-It* sheet per child
3 blank disks or tiles per child
1 disk or tile per child with <u>a</u>

Give the children three blank tiles and a tile with the letter <u>a</u> on it.

T: **Remember how we did this yesterday?**

T: **Watch me. It's my turn.**
Demonstrate *fan.* Show the children how to use the <u>a</u> tile again.

T: **Remember, you can use the <u>a</u> to show me where the /a/ sound should go.**

T: **Let's try it together. Ready?**
Practice again with the children, using the word *fan.*

T: **You can use the <u>a</u> if you want, or you can use just the blank tiles.**

at
ran
nab
/a/
man
as
rat

Teacher Notes for Lesson 21

Letter Name and Sound Instruction

Sound Bingo

You will need to photocopy from the **Materials Section** of the manual the Sound Bingo cards that reinforce a̲, m̲, t̲, i̲, and s̲. There are five different cards for today's version of the game. In a group of five, each child can have a different card.

Letter Name and Sound Instruction

Sound Bingo

Materials: 1 Sound Bingo card per child that reinforces <u>a</u>, <u>m</u>, <u>t</u>, <u>i</u>, and <u>s</u>

Copies of students' Sound Bingo cards, cut up and put in a box

1 handful of Bingo chips per child

1 die with letters on each side (for Option II)

Play using cards for letters <u>a</u>, <u>m</u>, <u>t</u>, <u>i</u>, and <u>s</u>. You may use either Option I or II as described in Lesson 7.

The following pictures are on the Sound Bingo cards:

<u>a</u> **pictures**	<u>m</u> **pictures**	<u>t</u> **pictures**
ambulance	money	telephone
ant	monkey	television
apple	moon	tiger
	mummy	turtle

<u>i</u> **pictures**	<u>s</u> **pictures**
igloo	Santa Claus
iguana	snake
insects	star

Teacher Notes for Lesson 21

Phonological Awareness Practice

Sound Categorization by Rhyme and Initial Sound

Remember, if the children have trouble with either rhyme or initial sound, just do one or the other.

Phonological Awareness Practice

Sound Categorization by Rhyme and Initial Sound

Materials: 4 sets of Sound Categorization by Rhyme cards
4 sets of Sound Categorization by Initial Sound cards

Repeat the procedure you used in Lesson 20, mixing sets of pictures that rhyme and sets of pictures that start with the same initial sound. Children must discover the rule (categorizing by rhyme or initial sound) for the set of pictures being used.

See Lessons 1 and 10 for complete descriptions of categorizing by rhyme or initial sound.

Teacher Notes for Lesson 22

Proper pacing is crucial!

Say-It-and-Move-It

Remember to modify the lesson for children who may not be ready for letters on their tiles (disks, blocks, or buttons). You might give them a letter tile during the demonstration so that they can practice, but remind all the children that they can always use just their blank tiles during *Say-It-and-Move-It*.

LESSON 22

Say-It-and-Move-It

Materials: 1 *Say-It-and-Move-It* sheet per child
3 blank disks or tiles per child
1 disk or tile per child with <u>m</u>

Give children three blank tiles and a tile with <u>m</u>.

T: **What do we have on the tiles today? Right. <u>m</u>.**

T: **Watch me. I'll show you how to use the <u>m</u> tile.**
Demonstrate using *mat* and *ram*.

T: **When you say it and move it, you can use the <u>m</u> tile if you think you know where it goes. You can also use all blank tiles.**

/m/
rim
am
mad
map
Sam
mop

Teacher Notes for Lesson 22

Letter Name and Sound Instruction

Go Fish

If you played this game with your children in Lesson 18, then you have already made multiple copies of each of the small, plain alphabet cards for the letters a, m, t, and i. Now you need to make multiple copies of the letter s to add to the game. The small, plain alphabet cards are in the **Materials Section** of the manual. Remember, it will help if you laminate each letter or paste it onto poster board.

Phonological Awareness Practice

Elkonin Cards

If you have not already made copies of all of the Elkonin cards, you will need to make copies of each of those cards that you need in this lesson. You will need one set for yourself and one set for every child in the group.

Remember to make sure the children can identify each picture before you ask them to segment.

Letter Name and Sound Instruction

Go Fish

Materials: Small, plain alphabet cards of <u>a</u>, <u>m</u>, <u>t</u>, <u>i</u>, and <u>s</u>
(multiple copies, see **Teacher Notes**)

Play with letter cards for <u>a</u>, <u>m</u>, <u>t</u>, <u>i</u>, and <u>s</u>.

See Lesson 18 for directions.

Phonological Awareness Practice

Elkonin Cards

Materials: Elkonin cards: fat, jam, sit, web, ram (1 per child)
3 disks or tiles per child

Give each child three blank tiles, and follow the procedure
described in Lesson 13 using the following pictures:

fat
jam
sit
web
ram

Teacher Notes for Lesson 23

Say-It-and-Move-It

Please note that this is the first time we will be using a stop consonant (e.g., /t/) in the initial position during the *Say-It-and-Move-It* activity. Remember that stop consonants need to be said quickly, so you won't be able to elongate or hold the first sound as we have been doing in all the past lessons. That also means the first tile has to be moved quickly while saying the stop consonant fast. You might want to tell the children that sounds like /t/ are "hot sounds." You need to say the "hot sounds" fast, and then get off of them quickly.

LESSON 23

Say-It-and-Move-It

Materials: 1 *Say-It-and-Move-It* sheet per child
3 blank disks or tiles per child
1 disk or tile per child with t

Give the children three blank tiles and a tile with t.

T: **What do we have on the tiles today? Right. t. I might trick you today. Some of the words will not have the /t/ sound. If you don't hear the /t/ sound in a word, be sure to use only blanks.**

T: **Watch me first.**
Demonstrate for the children, using the words *top, it,* and *man.* Repeat the demonstration using the same words and having the children try them with you.

T: **We didn't hear the /t/ sound in *man,* so we used only blanks.**

T: **You may use the t tile or the blank tiles.**

top
rat
ram
it
sat
Al
tab

Teacher Notes for Lesson 23

Letter Name and Sound Instruction

Introducing the Letter r

Remember that even though you are introducing a new letter, you should continue to review all of the previous letter names, letter sounds, and jingles.

Concentration

To play this simple matching game, you will need to make at least two copies of the small, plain alphabet cards for the letters a, m, t, i, and s that you will find in the **Materials Section** of the manual. If you played this game with your children in Lesson 14, you will have already started to collect the cards you need for Concentration. Now you can add multiple copies of the s card to your set of cards.

Letter Name and Sound Instruction

Introducing the Letter r

Materials: Large alphabet picture card of r

Using the r alphabet picture card, introduce r and the jingle:

red rooster in red running shoes

You might want to suggest names for the rooster beginning with r (Richard, Ronnie, Robert, Rudy, Raymond, Ricky, Ralph, Rufus, Randy, Rupert). If the children question the lack of female names, remind them that roosters are male animals.

Concentration

Materials: Small, plain alphabet cards of a, m, t, i, and s (multiple pairs, see **Teacher Notes**)

Play using small, plain alphabet cards for a, m, t, i, and s.

See Lesson 14 for directions.

Teacher Notes for Lesson 23

Phonological Awareness Practice

Post Office

To prepare for this game, you will need five brown lunch bags. Photocopy the small alphabet picture cards (for today's game use the <u>a</u>, <u>m</u>, <u>t</u>, <u>i</u>, and <u>s</u> small alphabet picture cards) from the **Materials Section** of the manual, and tape or use a glue stick to affix one card to the front of each lunch bag. Stand the bags up on the table in front of the children.

You will also need three or four pictures of objects that start with each of the sounds in today's lesson. You can photocopy the Sound Bingo cards found in the **Materials Section** and use the pictures as the items to be "mailed," or you can use other sources to gather pictures. If you use the cut-up Sound Bingo cards, you might want to laminate them or paste each picture onto poster board to make the materials last longer.

Phonological Awareness Practice

Post Office

Materials: Small alphabet picture cards of <u>a</u>, <u>m</u>, <u>t</u>, <u>i</u>, and <u>s</u>
Brown lunch bags
Pictures of objects that start with /a/, /m/, /t/, /i/, and /s/
Large canvas bag or shopping bag designated as letter carrier's bag

To Play: In this game, children will isolate and identify the first sound of words that begin with /a/, /m/, /t/, /i/, and /s/. Players assume the role of letter carrier and deliver the "mail" (pictures) to the appropriate "mailboxes" (lunch bags with small alphabet picture cards pasted to the front of each bag).

Begin by placing all the pictures to be used that day into the letter carrier's bag. The children take turns being the letter carrier. The letter carrier reaches into the bag and pulls out a picture. He or she then names the pictured object, gives the initial sound of the object, and delivers it to the appropriate mailbox by putting it into the lunch bag that is labeled with the letter that represents the first sound of the pictured object. The letter carrier's bag is then passed to the next child who assumes the role of letter carrier. When all of the "mail" has been delivered, the mailboxes can be checked to see whether the mail was delivered to the correct mailboxes.

Teacher Notes for Lesson 24

Say-It-and-Move-It

Remember, children are ready to use a particular letter tile when they can automatically associate the letter name and letter sound.

LESSON 24

Say-It-and-Move-It

Materials: 1 *Say-It-and-Move-It* sheet per child
3 blank disks or tiles per child
1 disk or tile per child with <u>a</u>

Give the children three blank tiles and a tile with <u>a</u>. Remember, if some children aren't ready to use the letter tile, they can continue to use blanks.

T: **What do we have on the tiles today? Yes. <u>a</u>.**

T: **Let's see if you remember how I tried to trick you yesterday. Yes, I gave you some words that did not have the sound that was on the tile, and you had to use only blanks.**

T: **Today we'll play that game again. This time, some of the words will not have the /a/ sound. When you hear /a/, you can use the special tile, and if you don't hear /a/, use only blanks.**

am
rat
rim
mat
/a/
set
mop
as

Teacher Notes for Lesson 24

Letter Name and Sound Instruction

Phonological Awareness Practice

Let's Fish!

If you played this game with your children in Lesson 15, then you have already made the fishing pole (a dowel-like stick with a string and magnet attached to one end) and collected some of the pictures to use as "fish." Remember that you can use pictures from the Sound Bingo games in this manual by photocopying the Sound Bingo cards, cutting them up, and laminating the individual pictures or pasting them individually onto poster board. Then put a piece of magnetic tape on the back or attach a paper clip so that the fish can be caught by the magnet on the fishing pole.

If you chose not to introduce Let's Fish! in an earlier lesson and don't have these materials available, substitute one of the other phonological awareness games that your students have enjoyed.

Letter Name and Sound Instruction

Review

Materials: List of jingles
Small, plain alphabet cards of <u>a</u>, <u>m</u>, <u>t</u>, <u>i</u>, <u>s</u>, and <u>r</u>

Review the sounds for the letters <u>a</u>, <u>m</u>, <u>t</u>, <u>i</u>, <u>s</u>, and <u>r</u>.

Have the children take turns being the teacher.

Give one small, plain alphabet card to each child. (The children can keep them face down, if they wish, until it is their turn to be the teacher.) Taking turns, each child becomes the teacher and calls on another child in the group to give the letter name and sound of the card the "teaching" child holds up. The "teaching" child can also request the jingle for each letter.

Each child should have a turn being the teacher, and each child in the group should be called on an equal number of times.

Phonological Awareness Practice

Let's Fish!

Materials: Fishing pole
4 "fish" representing each of the sounds being reviewed: /a/, /m/, /t/, /i/, /s/, and /r/

The pictured objects that you use as "fish" should begin with the /a/, /m/, /t/, /i/, /s/, and /r/ sounds. (Remember, we are using only the short sounds of the vowels.)

See Lesson 15 for directions.

Teacher Notes for Lesson 25

Say-It-and-Move-It

Remember, if you are using only blank tiles with your children, you will need to alter the lesson script accordingly.

LESSON 25

Say-It-and-Move-It

Materials: 1 *Say-It-and-Move-It* sheet per child
3 blank disks or tiles per child
1 disk or tile per child with i

Give the children three blank tiles and a tile with i.

T: **What do we have on the tiles today? Yes. i.**

T. **Let's see if you remember how I tried to trick you yesterday. Yes, I gave you some words that did not have the sound that was on the tile, and you had to use only blanks.**

T: **Today we'll play that game again. This time some of the words will not have the /i/ sound. When you hear /i/, you can use the special tile, and if you don't hear /i/, use only blanks.**

/i/
it
sit
an
ran
lip
rub
in

Teacher Notes for Lesson 25

Letter Name and Sound Instruction

Alphabet Books

To prepare for this lesson, make photocopies of the large alphabet picture card of the letter r so that each child will have a copy to color. All of the children will need red crayons to color the red rooster in red running shoes.

Letter Name and Sound Instruction

Alphabet Books

Materials: Alphabet books
1 large alphabet picture card per child of r
Crayons (each child should get a red crayon)

Give each child a large alphabet picture card of the letter r to color. You may want to repeat the jingle **"red rooster in red running shoes"** so the children will be cued to color the rooster and the running shoes red.

When the children are finished coloring, go through the book and review the letter names, letter sounds, and jingles.

Teacher Notes for Lesson 25

Phonological Awareness Practice

Save the Rabbit

In this new game we are introducing today, you will notice that we are including more opportunities to associate the sounds of letters with their printed symbols. As the children gain more knowledge of letter sound associations, more of the games reinforce this knowledge. So although we want the children to guess the mystery word primarily by thinking about the sounds in the word (e.g., isolating the initial and last sounds), this game also reinforces letter sound associations. As such, this game could also be included in our *Letter Name and Sound Instruction* category because it combines phonological awareness *and* awareness of the printed symbols that represent the spoken sounds.

To prepare for this new game, you need only a chalkboard or dry erase board, chalk or appropriate markers, and small pieces of paper.

Phonological Awareness Practice

Save the Rabbit

Materials: Chalkboard or dry erase board
Chalk or appropriate markers
Small pieces of paper
Box or other container

To Play: This game is played like the game of Hangman. The object of the game is to guess the mystery word before the entire rabbit is erased. If the word is guessed in time, the rabbit is saved.

Select a mystery word and write it on a piece of paper. Place the paper in a box or other container. Next, draw a series of dashes on the board. There is one dash for each letter in the word. For example, if the mystery word is *mat,* you would draw _ _ _ on the board. Then say, **"These are the sounds we will be using: /a/, /m/, /t/, /i/, and /s/."** As you say each sound, list its corresponding letter on the board. Next, draw a rabbit next to the list of sounds.

For example, in today's lesson you are going to use the sounds /a/, /m/, /t/, /i/, and /s/. The board would look like the drawing on the next page.

Teacher Notes for Lesson 25

The first player chooses one of the sounds listed on the board. If the chosen sound is in the mystery word, you write the letter that represents that sound on the appropriate line. Then put a slash through the letter in the list so the children know not to guess that letter's sound again. If the chosen sound is *not* in the mystery word, erase one part of the rabbit (e.g., an ear) and draw a slash through the incorrect letter in the list.

When one or more sounds have been correctly chosen to fill in the blanks (e.g., m _ t), encourage the children to think of a word that, for example, begins with /m/ and ends with /t/.

When the mystery word has been guessed correctly, show the children the word that was written on a piece of paper and placed in the box or container before the game began. Have them compare it with the word on the board. This way the children can see that they have, in fact, guessed the mystery word.

Teacher Notes for Lesson 26

Say-It-and-Move-It

LESSON 26

Say-It-and-Move-It

Materials: 1 *Say-It-and-Move-It* sheet per child
3 blank disks or tiles per child
1 disk or tile per child with <u>s</u>

Give the children three blank tiles and a tile with <u>s</u>.

T: **What letter is on our tile today? Yes. <u>s</u>.**

T: **We have some new words to practice, so you will have to listen very carefully! Be sure to listen for the /s/ sound.**

T: **Are you ready? Fingers in the air?**

yes
van
sob
/e/
sip
gas
us
let

Teacher Notes for Lesson 26

Letter Name and Sound Instruction

Go Fish

As instructed in Lesson 18, to prepare for this game you need multiple copies of the small, plain alphabet cards found in the **Materials Section** of the manual. With six letters, four to six copies of each letter should be adequate for a group of four children.

Phonological Awareness Practice

Elkonin Cards

You will notice in this lesson that we use stop consonants (e.g., p̲) in the initial position in some of the words (e.g., p̲in) that the children are segmenting on the Elkonin cards. Remind the children that those are "hot sounds" and we get off of them quickly.

If you have not already made copies of all of the Elkonin cards, you will need to make a copy of each Elkonin card used in this lesson for each child.

We also want to remind you that if you like a particular activity and it works well for your group, you might want to use that activity more often. Substitute it for one of the other activities in the *Phonological Awareness Practice* category. For example, Save the Rabbit is one of the more challenging *Phonological Awareness Practice* activities. You may want to use that activity in place of Elkonin Cards or other games we suggest.

Letter Name and Sound Instruction

Go Fish

Materials: Small, plain alphabet cards of <u>a</u>, <u>m</u>, <u>t</u>, <u>i</u>, <u>s</u>, and <u>r</u> (multiple pairs, see **Teacher Notes**)

Play using cards for letters <u>a</u>, <u>m</u>, <u>t</u>, <u>i</u>, <u>s</u>, and <u>r</u>.

See Lesson 18 for directions.

Phonological Awareness Practice

Elkonin Cards

Materials: Elkonin cards: pin, jet, bag, pot, jug (1 per child)
3 disks or tiles per child

For this lesson give the children three blank tiles, and use the following Elkonin cards:

pin
jet
bag
pot
jug

See Lesson 13 for directions.

Teacher Notes for Lesson 27

Say-It-and-Move-It

Remember that the children should have either three blank tiles and a letter tile **or** four blank tiles.

LESSON 27

Say-It-and-Move-It

Materials: 1 *Say-It-and-Move-It* sheet per child
3 blank disks or tiles per child
1 disk or tile per child with i

Give the children three blank tiles and a tile with i.

T: **What letter is on our tile today? Yes. i.**

T: **We have some new words to practice, so you will have to listen very carefully! Be sure to listen for the /i/ sound.**

T: **Are you ready? Fingers in the air?**

zip
/o/
rib
if
mat
in
pin
nut

Teacher Notes for Lesson 27

Letter Name and Sound Instruction

Review

A list of jingles can be found in the **Materials Section** of the manual.

As we have indicated earlier, it is important to periodically assess the letter name and sound knowledge of each child in your group. In Lesson 29, another new letter will be introduced, so it would be a good idea to assess knowledge of the letter names and letter sounds taught thus far, before you get to Lesson 29.

Phonological Awareness Practice

Let's Fish!

If you played Let's Fish! in Lesson 24, you will find that this lesson reviews the same sounds. Consequently, you won't need any new materials.

If you have not made the materials to play this game, feel free to substitute any of the other games you have played in this category in previous lessons.

Letter Name and Sound Instruction

Review

Materials: List of jingles
Large alphabet picture cards of <u>a</u>, <u>m</u>, <u>t</u>, <u>i</u>, <u>s</u>, and <u>r</u>

Review the letter names and sounds for <u>a</u>, <u>m</u>, <u>t</u>, <u>i</u>, <u>s</u>, and <u>r</u>, using the large alphabet picture cards. Have the children give the letter name, letter sound, and jingle for each.

Phonological Awareness Practice

Let's Fish!

Materials: Fishing pole
4 "fish" representing each of the sounds being reviewed: /a/, /m/, /t/, /i/, /s/, and /r/

The pictured objects you will use as "fish" should begin with /a/, /m/, /t/, /i/, /s/, and /r/.

See Lesson 15 for directions.

Teacher Notes for Lesson 28

Say-It-and-Move-It

Letter Name and Sound Instruction

LESSON 28

Say-It-and-Move-It

Materials: 1 *Say-It-and-Move-It* sheet per child
3 blank disks or tiles per child
1 disk or tile per child with <u>m</u>

Give children three blank tiles and one with an <u>m</u>.

T: **What letter is on our tile today? Yes. <u>m</u>.**

T: **We have some new words to practice today, so listen very carefully. Be sure to listen for the /m/ sound.**

T: **Are you ready? Fingers in the air?**

fed
mop
am
rim
rug
mad

Letter Name and Sound Instruction

I'm Thinking of a Word

Materials: Large alphabet picture cards of <u>a</u>, <u>m</u>, <u>t</u>, <u>i</u>, <u>s</u>, and <u>r</u>

Use alphabet picture cards of <u>a</u>, <u>m</u>, <u>t</u>, <u>i</u>, <u>s</u>, and <u>r</u>.

See Lesson 8 for directions.

Teacher Notes for Lesson 28

Phonological Awareness Practice

Sound Categorization by Rhyme and Initial Sound

When you select sets for categorization, you might want to include a rhyming set and an initial sound set that share at least one picture. For example, *cat* can be grouped with *fat* and *mat* in a rhyming set or with *cap* and *cup* in an initial sound set. This will help the children see that the same word can be classified in more than one way.

Phonological Awareness Practice

Sound Categorization by Rhyme and Initial Sound

Materials: 4 sets of Sound Categorization by Rhyme cards
4 sets of Sound Categorization by Initial Sound cards

See Lesson 20 for directions.

Teacher Notes for Lesson 29

Say-It-and-Move-It

LESSON 29

Say-It-and-Move-It

Materials: 1 *Say-It-and-Move-It* sheet per child
3 blank disks or tiles per child
1 disk or tile per child with <u>s</u>

Give the children three blank tiles and a tile with <u>s</u>.

T: **What letter is on our tile today? Yes. <u>s</u>.**

T: **Listen carefully for the words that have the /s/ sound.**

T: **Are you ready? Fingers in the air?**

sip
us
rap
yes
sun
sap
in
sub

Teacher Notes for Lesson 29

Letter Name and Sound Instruction

Introducing the Letter b̲

You might want to color your copy of the large alphabet picture card of b̲ before introducing it to the children. Remember that the b̲ is a stop consonant. When you pronounce it, be sure to say it fast (it also helps if you whisper the sound) so it is distorted as little as possible.

Letter Name and Sound Instruction

Introducing the Letter b

Materials: Large alphabet picture card of b

Using the b alphabet picture, introduce the letter name, letter sound, and jingle:

big boy bouncing on the bed

Repeat the phrase several times. Then ask the students to put a finger up every time they hear the /b/ sound.

Next, you might want to suggest names for the boy beginning with the /b/ sound (e.g., Buddy, Bobby, Ben, Billy, Bert). Let the children suggest other names. Then give each child one of the names to remember.

Use the following song:

"Who's the big boy bouncing on the bed?"

Repeat the song for each child. The child will say, "It's ____ (the name assigned to the child), that's who!"

For example:

| Teacher: | **Who's the big boy bouncing on the bed?** |
| Child: | **It's Bobby, that's who!** |

Teacher Notes for Lesson 29

Sound Bingo

You will need to photocopy from the **Materials Section** of the manual the Sound Bingo cards that reinforce <u>a</u>, <u>m</u>, <u>t</u>, <u>i</u>, <u>s</u>, and <u>r</u>. As always, there are five different cards for today's version of the game. In a group of five, each child can have a different card.

You will note there are more of certain letters on some of the individual Sound Bingo cards. If a child is having trouble with a particular sound, give that child the Sound Bingo card with more of that letter.

Sound Bingo

Materials: 1 Sound Bingo card per child that reinforces <u>a</u>, <u>m</u>, <u>t</u>, <u>i</u>, <u>s</u>, and <u>r</u>

Copies of students' Sound Bingo cards, cut up and put in a box

1 handful of Bingo chips per child

1 die with letters on each side (for Option II)

Play using letters <u>a</u>, <u>m</u>, <u>t</u>, <u>i</u>, <u>s</u>, and <u>r</u>. You may use Option I or II.

The following pictures are on the Sound Bingo cards:

<u>a</u> **pictures**	<u>m</u> **pictures**	<u>t</u> **pictures**
ambulance	map	telephone
ant	milk	television
apple	mouse	tiger
		turtle

<u>i</u> **pictures**	<u>s</u> **pictures**	<u>r</u> **pictures**
igloo	Santa Claus	rabbit
iguana	snake	rain
insects	spider	reindeer
	star	runner

See Lesson 7 for directions.

Teacher Notes for Lesson 29

Phonological Awareness Practice

Phonological Awareness Practice

Elkonin Cards

Materials: Elkonin cards: tub, wag, hen, can, ten (1 per child)
3 disks or tiles per child

For this lesson give the children three blank tiles and use the following Elkonin cards:

tub
wag
hen
can
ten

See Lesson 13 for directions.

Teacher Notes for Lesson 30

Proper pacing is crucial!

Say-It-and-Move-It

Remember that not all children are ready to use letter tiles at the same point in time. We first introduced the letter tile <u>a</u> in Lesson 20. If some of your children were not ready in Lesson 20 because they could not automatically associate the letter name and sound, check to see whether they can automatically associate the letter name and sound at this point in the program. You might find that one or two more children are now ready to use letter tiles or that this is a good time to start using letter tiles with a whole group that was not ready earlier in the program.

Letter Name and Sound Instruction

Concentration

To prepare for this simple matching and memory game, you will need to make at least two copies of each of the small, plain alphabet cards for the letters <u>a</u>, <u>m</u>, <u>t</u>, <u>i</u>, <u>s</u>, <u>r</u>, and <u>b</u>. To make the game shorter, use only five of the letters.

LESSON 30

Say-It-and-Move-It

Materials: 1 *Say-It-and-Move-It* sheet per child
3 blank disks or tiles per child
1 disk or tile per child with <u>a</u>

Give the children three blank tiles and a tile with <u>a</u>.

T: **What letter is on our tile today? Yes. <u>a</u>.**

T: **We have some new words to practice, so you will have to listen very carefully! Be sure to listen for the /a/ sound.**

T: **Are you ready? Fingers in the air?**

as
sub
van
rap
us
ran

Letter Name and Sound Instruction

Concentration

Materials: Small, plain alphabet cards of <u>a</u>, <u>m</u>, <u>t</u>, <u>i</u>, <u>s</u>, <u>r</u>, and <u>b</u> (multiple pairs, see **Teacher Notes**)

Play using letters <u>a</u>, <u>m</u>, <u>t</u>, <u>i</u>, <u>s</u>, <u>r</u>, and <u>b</u>.

See Lesson 14 for directions.

Teacher Notes for Lesson 30

Phonological Awareness Practice

Post Office

To prepare for this lesson, you will need three or four pictures of objects that start with each of the sounds being reinforced. Remember, you can photocopy and cut up the Sound Bingo cards for use in this game.

Phonological Awareness Practice

Post Office

Materials: Small alphabet picture cards of <u>a</u>, <u>m</u>, <u>t</u>, <u>i</u>, <u>s</u>, and <u>r</u>
Brown lunch bags
Pictures of objects that start with /a/, /m/, /t/, /i/,
/s/, and /r/
Large canvas or shopping bag

Play by using lunch bags as "mailboxes" and pictures of objects that start with /a/, /m/, /t/, /i/, /s/, and /r/ sounds as "mail." You may use all six sounds or choose the sounds that need the most practice.

See Lesson 23 for directions.

Teacher Notes for Lesson 31

Say-It-and-Move-It

LESSON 31

Say-It-and-Move-It

Materials: 1 *Say-It-and-Move-It* sheet per child
3 blank disks or tiles per child
1 disk or tile per child with i

Give the children three blank tiles and a tile with i.

T: **What letter is on the tile today? Yes. i.**

T: **Listen carefully for the words that have the /i/ sound.**

T: **Are you ready? Fingers in the air?**

it
fin
if
rip
/u/
fat
tin

Teacher Notes for Lesson 31

Letter Name and Sound Instruction

Alphabet Books

To prepare for this lesson, make enough copies of the large alphabet picture card of the letter <u>b</u> so that each child has one to color.

Phonological Awareness Practice

Sound Categorization by Rhyme and Initial Sound

If the children are having difficulty alternating between words that start with the same initial sound and rhyming words, just work on groups of words that start with the same sound.

Letter Name and Sound Instruction

Alphabet Books

Materials: Alphabet books
1 large alphabet picture card per child of <u>b</u>
Crayons

Have each child color a large alphabet picture card of the letter <u>b</u>.

While they are coloring, talk about the letter <u>b</u>. What else starts with the letter <u>b</u>? See how many things the children can come up with.

Phonological Awareness Practice

Sound Categorization by Rhyme and Initial Sound

Materials: 4 sets of Sound Categorization by Rhyme cards
4 sets of Sound Categorization by Initial Sound cards

See Lesson 20 for directions.

Teacher Notes for Lesson 32

Say-It-and-Move-It

LESSON 32

Say-It-and-Move-It

Materials: 1 *Say-It-and-Move-It* sheet per child
3 blank disks or tiles per child
1 disk or tile per child with <u>t</u>

Give children three blank tiles and a tile with <u>t</u>.

T: **Can you tell which sound we need to listen carefully for today? Yes. /t/.**

T: **Are you ready? Fingers in the air?**

/o/
it
jam
tin
tap
sip
tag

Teacher Notes for Lesson 32

Letter Name and Sound Instruction

Sound Boards

Each child will need an individual sound board (adapted from Beth Slingerland, 1971) for this activity. To facilitate the construction of these sound boards or pocket charts, we have provided a detailed description of how to make them in the **Materials Section** of the manual. Ideally, each child in the group will have a sound board, and you will have one for demonstration purposes. You can get started with just one, passing it from child to child. However, if each child has a sound board, this cuts down dramatically on "wait time," because each child can respond to each request from the teacher (e.g., "Show me the letter that makes the /m/ sound").

To construct the sound board, you need poster board, plastic tape, and felt-tipped red and black markers. Each sound board will look like this:

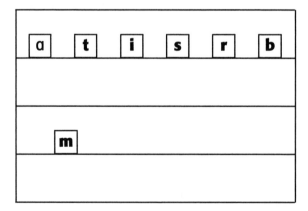

As you know, in this program we introduce only eight letters. That means you will need only eight letter cards for each child's sound board. However, if you think you will be using the sound board to work on other letters with your children, you might want to make a complete set of letter cards. We used permanent felt-tipped pens to write the letters on poster board. We wrote the consonants in black and the vowels in red.

Please note that you need to set up the sound boards for the children before you pass them out. That is, before the activity begins, you should put the letters the children will need that day in the top pocket of each sound board. Store the extra letters (or letters not being used in the les-

Letter Name and Sound Instruction

Sound Boards

Review **TEACHER NOTES** for this lesson before proceeding.

Materials: 1 sound board per child with <u>a</u>, <u>m</u>, <u>t</u>, <u>i</u>, <u>s</u>, <u>r</u>, and <u>b</u>

Introduce the sound board activity. The following letters should be in the upper pocket: <u>a</u>, <u>m</u>, <u>t</u>, <u>i</u>, <u>s</u>, <u>r</u>, and <u>b</u>.

T: **Today we are going to be using these sound boards.**

T: **When I ask you to show me a letter, I want you to take the letter out and put it in the bottom pocket.**

T: **For example, if I say, "Show me <u>a</u>," this is what I want you to do.**
Demonstrate for the children.

T: **Now it's your turn.**

T: **Show me <u>m</u>. Good.**

T: **What sound does <u>m</u> make? /m/. Good.**

T: **Show me the letter that makes the /m/ sound. <u>m</u>. Good.**
Follow the same procedure for each letter. You may alternate the process by giving the sound first.

Teacher Notes for Lesson 32

son) in an envelope or Ziploc bag. These may be taped to the back of the sound board.

Phonological Awareness Practice

Let's Fish!

Remember that to play this game you need a pole with string and a magnet attached to it. You also need to put magnetic tape or a paper clip on each picture.

Phonological Awareness Practice

Let's Fish!

Materials: Fishing pole
4 "fish" representing each of the sounds being
reviewed: /a/, /m/, /t/, /i/, /s/, and /r/

The pictured objects you use as "fish" should begin with the /a/, /m/, /t/, /i/, /s/, and /r/ sounds.

See Lesson 15 for directions.

Teacher Notes for Lesson 33

Say-It-and-Move-It

LESSON 33

Say-It-and-Move-It

Materials: 1 *Say-It-and-Move-It* sheet per child
3 blank disks or tiles per child
1 disk or tile per child with <u>s</u>

Give the children three blank tiles and a tile with <u>s</u>.

T: **Can you tell which sound we need to listen carefully for today? Yes. /s/.**

T: **Are you ready? Fingers in the air?**

an
sob
yes
sun
sag
gas
mat

Teacher Notes for Lesson 33

Letter Name and Sound Instruction

Sound Bingo

You will need to photocopy from the **Materials Section** of the manual the Sound Bingo cards that reinforce <u>a</u>, <u>i</u>, <u>s</u>, <u>r</u>, and <u>b</u>. As always, there are five different cards for today's version of the game. In a group of five, each child can have a different card.

Letter Name and Sound Instruction

Sound Bingo

Materials: 1 Sound Bingo card per child that reinforces <u>a</u>, <u>i</u>, <u>s</u>, <u>r</u>, and <u>b</u>

Copies of students' Sound Bingo cards, cut up and put in a box

1 handful of Bingo chips per child

1 die with letters on each side (for Option II)

Play using letters <u>a</u>, <u>i</u>, <u>s</u>, <u>r</u>, and <u>b</u>. Use either Option I or II.

See Lesson 7 for directions.

The following pictures are on the Sound Bingo cards:

<u>a</u> pictures	**<u>i</u> pictures**	**<u>s</u> pictures**
ambulance	igloo	Santa Claus
ant	insects	snake
		star

<u>r</u> pictures	**<u>b</u> pictures**
rabbit	ballerina
rain	balloon (hot air)
reindeer	bananas
runner	bat and ball
	birthday cake

Teacher Notes for Lesson 33

Phonological Awareness Practice

Save the Rabbit

To prepare for this game, you need only a chalkboard or dry erase board, chalk or appropriate markers, small pieces of paper, and a box or other container.

Phonological Awareness Practice

Save the Rabbit

Materials: Chalkboard or dry erase board
Chalk or appropriate markers
Small pieces of paper
Box or other container

Play using the following sounds: /a/, /m/, /t/, /s/, and /r/. As you say each sound, list its corresponding letter on the board. Draw a rabbit next to the list of sounds, as illustrated in Lesson 25.

See Lesson 25 for directions.

Teacher Notes for Lesson 34

Say-It-and-Move-It

Letter Name and Sound Instruction

Sound Boards

Remember to have the sound boards ready for the children. Before the lesson begins, place the letters they will need in the top pocket. Directions for preparing the sound boards are in the **Materials Section** of the manual, and additional suggestions for their use are in Lesson 32.

LESSON 34

Say-It-and-Move-It

Materials: 1 *Say-It-and-Move-It* sheet per child
3 blank disks or tiles per child
1 disk or tile per child with <u>r</u>

Give the children three blank tiles and a tile with <u>r</u>.

T: **Can you tell which sound we need to listen carefully for today? Yes. /r/.**

T: **Are you ready? Fingers in the air?**

/e/
as
run
tan
rob
rip
Al
red

Letter Name and Sound Instruction

Sound Boards

Materials: 1 sound board per child with <u>a</u>, <u>m</u>, <u>t</u>, <u>i</u>, <u>s</u>, <u>r</u>, and <u>b</u>

Give each child a sound board, as you did in Lesson 32. The following letters should be in the top pocket: <u>a</u>, <u>m</u>, <u>t</u>, <u>i</u>, <u>s</u>, <u>r</u>, and <u>b</u>.

Teacher Notes for Lesson 34

Phonological Awareness Practice

Post Office

To prepare for this lesson, you will need three or four pictures of objects that start with each of the sounds being reinforced. Remember, you can photocopy and cut up the Sound Bingo cards for use in this game.

T: **Today we are going to use our sound boards again.**

T: **When I ask you to show me a letter, I want you to take the letter out and put it in the bottom pocket.**

T: **For example, if I say, "Show me <u>a</u>," this is what I want you to do.**
Demonstrate for the children.

T: **Now it's your turn.**

T: **Show me <u>m.</u> Good.**

T: **What sound does <u>m</u> make? /m/. Good.**
Do the same for each letter. You may give the sound first.

Phonological Awareness Practice

Post Office

Materials: Small alphabet picture cards of <u>m</u>, <u>t</u>, <u>i</u>, <u>s</u>, <u>r</u>, and <u>b</u>
Brown lunch bags
Pictures of objects that start with /m/, /t/, /i/, /s/, /r/, and /b/
Large canvas or shopping bag

Play by using lunch bags as "mailboxes" and pictures of objects that start with /m/, /t/, /i/, /s/, /r/, and /b/ as "mail." You may use all six sounds or choose the sounds that need the most practice.

See Lesson 23 for directions.

Teacher Notes for Lesson 35

Say-It-and-Move-It

As you will notice, we are introducing an additional blank tile today. We want to make the activity more challenging by requiring the children to select the correct number of tiles, disks, or blocks to use from a larger set of manipulatives.

Letter Name and Sound Instruction

Remember, as we discussed before starting Lesson 1, in the 44 lessons in this manual we have chosen to introduce only eight letters. This is the last lesson in which we introduce a new letter name and letter sound. This does not mean that we think these are the only letter sounds that children need to learn. Depending on the skill levels of your children and their success with the eight letters introduced so far, you may want to introduce additional letters during the next nine lessons.

Proper pacing is crucial!

LESSON 35

Say-It-and-Move-It

Materials: 1 *Say-It-and-Move-It* sheet per child
4 blank disks or tiles per child
1 disk or tile per child with i̲

Give the children four blank tiles and a tile with i̲.

T: **Can you tell which sound we need to listen carefully for today? Yes. /i/.**

T: **Are you ready? Fingers in the air?**

it
jam
lit
rip
in
sub
bit

Letter Name and Sound Instruction

Introducing the Letter f̲

Materials: Large alphabet picture card of f̲

Using the f̲ large alphabet picture card, introduce the letter name, letter sound, and jingle:

f̲ive f̲unny f̲aces

Teacher Notes for Lesson 35

Phonological Awareness Practice

Alphabet Books

Materials: Alphabet books

Give the children their alphabet books, and review the letter names and sounds for <u>a</u>, <u>m</u>, <u>t</u>, <u>i</u>, <u>s</u>, <u>r</u>, and <u>b</u>.

Phonological Awareness Practice

Sound Categorization by Rhyme and Initial Sound

Materials: 4 sets of Sound Categorization by Rhyme cards
4 sets of Sound Categorization by Initial Sound cards

Try mixing initial sounds and rhyming sets as you have done in previous lessons. You may want to start with two sets of initial sound pictures and ask how they are the same. Then use two sets of rhyming cards. Try to get the children to verbalize that the initial sound sets are the same because they have the same beginning sounds. The rhyming sets match because they are the same at the end. Then mix the sets and see whether the children can pick the odd one out and give the rule.

See Lesson 20 for directions.

Teacher Notes for Lesson 36

Proper pacing is crucial!

Say-It-and-Move-It

If you have been using blank tiles with all of your children, you might want to reassess their readiness for letter tiles before introducing this lesson. Review Lesson 20 for directions on how to introduce letter tiles.

If, on the other hand, you are working with children who are quite successful using one letter tile, you might try increasing the difficulty of the lesson by introducing two letter tiles. For example, in this lesson, you could give the children a tile with an <u>s</u> on it and a tile with a <u>b</u> on it. Use the word *sub* to demonstrate with your tiles how to say it and move it with two letter tiles. Then repeat the example, having the children move their tiles as you move your tiles.

In Lessons 37, 39, 40, 42, and 43, you will find suggestions for trying two letter tiles with those children who are ready.

LESSON 36

Say-It-and-Move-It

Materials: 1 *Say-It-and-Move-It* sheet per child
4 blank disks or tiles per child
1 disk or tile per child with <u>b</u>

Review **TEACHER NOTES** for this lesson before proceeding.

Be sure to read the new letter tile suggestions in the Teacher Notes.

Give the children four blank tiles and a tile with <u>b</u>.

T: **Can you tell which sound we need to listen carefully for today? Yes. /b/.**

T: **Are you ready? Fingers in the air?**

/u/
bus
sub
bet
rub
us
bin
sob

Teacher Notes for Lesson 36

Letter Name and Sound Instruction

Sound Boards

Remember to have the sound boards ready for the children by placing the letters they will need in the top pocket.

Letter Name and Sound Instruction

Sound Boards

Materials: 1 sound board per child with <u>a</u>, <u>m</u>, <u>t</u>, <u>s</u>, <u>r</u>, <u>b</u>, and <u>f</u>

Give each child a sound board with the letters <u>a</u>, <u>m</u>, <u>t</u>, <u>s</u>, <u>r</u>, <u>b</u>, and <u>f</u> in the top pocket.

Review the names and sounds of each letter as you did in Lesson 32.

Tell the children:

T: **Today we are going to do something different. We are going to put letters together to make words.**

T: **Watch me. I want to make *at*.**

T: **How many sounds are in *at*? Two. Good.**

T: **How many letters will I need then? Two. Good.**

T: **Which sound comes first?**
Repeat the word, saying it slowly.
/aaat/.

T: **The /a/ sound. Right.**

T: **I will put it first.**
Move the <u>a</u> letter card down to the bottom pocket.

T: **Listen again. *At*. What sound comes next? /t/. Good.**

T: **What word did I make? *At*. Good.**
Sweep your finger under the word and repeat the word.

Teacher Notes for Lesson 36

Phonological Awareness Practice

Let's Fish!

Remember that to play this game you need a pole with string and a magnet attached to it. You also need to put magnetic tape or a paper clip on each picture.

T: **Now it's your turn to make words.**

T: **Get ready.**

Help the children make *at* by having them move their letter cards as you model with your sound board. When everyone has *at* on the board, say,

T: **Let's make *at* into *bat*. Watch me. *At*.**
Move <u>b</u> in front of *at*.

T: ***Bat*.**

Return the <u>b</u> to the top pocket and repeat, having the children move their <u>b</u> letter card in front of *at* as you model with your sound board. Then follow the same procedure and make *fat, rat, mat,* and *sat*. If children have difficulty, model again as described above.

Phonological Awareness Practice

Let's Fish!

Materials: Fishing pole
"Fish" representing each of the sounds that need
to be reviewed

This is a good chance to work on the sounds that are still giving the children trouble. Review your most recent letter name and sound assessments to determine which sounds need to be targeted for individual children. Choose the sounds that need the most practice, and use pictures of objects that begin with those sounds.

See Lesson 15 for directions.

Teacher Notes for Lesson 37

Say-It-and-Move-It

Remember that the children can continue to use all blank tiles if they have not mastered the sound on the letter tile that you are using in a particular lesson.

As described in the **Teacher Notes** in Lesson 36, you can also make lessons more challenging for those who are ready by introducing two letter tiles in one lesson. Today you could try m and r. Use only the eight letters we have introduced in this program.

Letter Name and Sound Instruction

Sound Boards

You will notice in these first sound board activities that we include only one vowel sound, the /a/ sound as in *apple*. Before asking children to change the vowel (e.g., making *fat* into *fit*), we want them to have practice changing initial sounds (e.g., *rat* into *bat*) and changing final sounds (e.g., *rat* into *ram*). In these early lessons, we introduce sound changes slowly, providing lots of practice changing initial sounds (e.g., *rat* into *bat*).

LESSON 37

Say-It-and-Move-It

Materials: 1 *Say-It-and-Move-It* sheet per child
4 blank disks or tiles per child
1 disk or tile per child with <u>m</u>

Give the children four blank tiles and a tile with <u>m</u>.

T: **Can you tell which sound we need to listen carefully for today? Yes. /m/.**

T: **Are you ready? Fingers in the air?**

am
ram
rib
mop
Ed
man
rim

Letter Name and Sound Instruction

Sound Boards

Materials: 1 sound board per child with <u>a</u>, <u>m</u>, <u>t</u>, <u>s</u>, <u>r</u>, <u>b</u>, and <u>f</u>

Give each child a sound board with the letters <u>a</u>, <u>m</u>, <u>t</u>, <u>s</u>, <u>r</u>, <u>b</u>, and <u>f</u> in the top pocket. Review the name and sound of each letter.

Teacher Notes for Lesson 37

There may be wide variation in how well kindergarten children do with simple word building on the sound board. Some children may be able to change initial sounds at the end of the 44 lessons, whereas others will be able to change initial, last, and middle sounds. It is easy to individualize using the sound board because you can ask individual children to make word changes (*at* into *bat*) that are matched to their skill level. We will give specific examples of this in Lesson 39.

Phonological Awareness Practice

Post Office

To prepare for today's lesson, you will need three or four pictures of objects that start with each of the sounds being reinforced. Remember, you can photocopy and cut up the Sound Bingo cards for this game.

Help the children spell *at* as you did in Lesson 36. Start with the letter that makes the /a/ sound, and ask the children how to make it into *at*. Then make *at* into *sat, mat, bat,* and *rat.* If the children did well with this pattern yesterday and you don't feel they need to repeat it, try this new pattern instead: *am, ram, am, at, rat, bat, fat.*

Phonological Awareness Practice

Post Office

Materials: Small alphabet picture cards of <u>m</u>, <u>s</u>, <u>r</u>, <u>b</u>, and <u>f</u>
Brown lunch bags
Pictures of objects that start with /m/, /s/, /r/, /b/, and /f/
Large canvas or shopping bag

Play by using lunch bags as "mailboxes" and pictures of objects that start with /m/, /s/, /r/, /b/, and /f/ as "mail." You may use all six of these sounds or select the sounds that need the most practice.

See Lesson 23 for directions.

Teacher Notes for Lesson 38

Say-It-and-Move-It

LESSON 38

Say-It-and-Move-It

Materials: 1 *Say-It-and-Move-It* sheet per child
4 blank disks or tiles per child
1 disk or tile per child with <u>t</u>

Give children four blank tiles and a tile with <u>t</u>.

T: **Can you tell which sound we need to listen carefully for today? Yes. /t/.**

T: **Are you ready? Fingers in the air?**

lit
bit
sag
hot
tip
met
/o/

Teacher Notes for Lesson 38

Letter Name and Sound Instruction

Alphabet Books

To prepare for this lesson, make enough copies of the large alphabet picture card of the letter f̲ so that each child has one to color.

Phonological Awareness Practice

Letter Name and Sound Instruction

Alphabet Books

Materials: Alphabet books
1 large alphabet picture card per child of f
Crayons

Have the children color the f alphabet picture card. Talk about each picture, and ask the children to think of other things that start with f.

Phonological Awareness Practice

Save the Rabbit

Materials: Chalkboard or dry erase board
Chalk or appropriate markers
Small pieces of paper
Box or other container

Play using the following sounds: /t/, /i/, /s/, /b/, and /f/.

See Lesson 25 for directions.

Teacher Notes for Lesson 39

Say-It-and-Move-It

If your children are ready to use two letter tiles, as discussed in the **Teacher Notes** in Lesson 36, try a and t tiles today. Remind your children that they will be listening carefully for two sounds.

LESSON 39

Say-It-and-Move-It

Materials: 1 *Say-It-and-Move-It* sheet per child
4 blank disks or tiles per child
1 disk or tile per child with <u>a</u>

Give the children four blank tiles and a tile with <u>a</u>.

T: **Which sound do you think we will listen for today?**

T: **Yes. /a/.**

T: **Are you ready? Fingers in the air?**

in
an
bat
pan
map
lot
at
rag

Teacher Notes for Lesson 39

Proper pacing is crucial!

Letter Name and Sound Instruction

Sound Boards

As we indicated earlier, we expect wide variation in what children are able to do in terms of word building with the sound board. One of the nice features of this activity is that it lends itself to individualization. It can be used to reinforce recognition of letter names and sounds (e.g., "Show me the t"; "Show me the letter that says /mmm/"), and it can be used for more advanced word building (e.g., make *bat* into *sat* into *sit*).

You may have children who are ready to use the sound board only as a tool to reinforce identification of single letter names and sounds, whereas other children may be ready to put words together. Remember, when building words, it is easiest to change the first sound (e.g., *fat* into *bat*), a bit more difficult to change the last sound (e.g., *rat* into *ram*), and most difficult to change the middle sound (e.g., *sat* into *sit*).

In this lesson, we provide one example of how to individualize for a group of children on at least three different levels. **Ultimately, you must select the sequence of words that is most appropriate for the children in your class.**

Letter Name and Sound Instruction

Sound Boards

Materials: 1 sound board per child with <u>a</u>, <u>m</u>, <u>t</u>, <u>r</u>, and <u>f</u>

The children will need the <u>a</u>, <u>m</u>, <u>t</u>, <u>r</u>, and <u>f</u> letters in the top pockets of their sound boards. Review the name and sound of each letter.

This sound board activity uses a patterned sequence of word building that makes it easy to individualize instruction for children at different ability levels.

<u>a</u>	Ask a child who still needs review of single sounds to put the letter that makes the /a/ sound in the lower pocket.
at	Ask a child who is at a beginning word building level to make /a/ into *at.*
fat	Ask a higher level child to make *at* into *fat.*
rat	Ask another higher level child to make *fat* into *rat.*
ram	Ask the *highest* level child to make *rat* into *ram.* (If you don't have anyone who can do this yet, just show the children how to make *rat* into *ram* on your sound board and go on to the next word.)
am	Ask a child who is at a beginning word building level to take one letter away to make *ram* into *am.*

Teacher Notes for Lesson 39

Phonological Awareness Practice

Sound Categorization by Rhyme and Initial Sound

Today when you use the Sound Categorization cards, select the *at* and *am* rhyming sets and the initial sound sets that use /b/ and /m/ in the initial position. You will also need the small, plain alphabet cards with the letters <u>a</u>, <u>m</u>, <u>t</u>, and <u>b</u> on them. As children group by rhyme or initial sound, use the alphabet cards to show them which letters the words have in common.

a   Ask a child who still needs review of single sounds to take one letter away from *am* to leave the letter that makes the /a/ sound.

Phonological Awareness Practice

Sound Categorization by Rhyme and Initial Sound

Materials: *At* and *am* Sound Categorization by Rhyme cards
               /b/ and /m/ Sound Categorization by Initial
                 Sound cards
               Small, plain alphabet cards of a, m, t, and b

Select *at* and *am* rhyming sets and initial sound sets that you can group by /b/ and /m/. As the children identify the words that rhyme or begin with the same sound, help them articulate the rule and identify the letters that represent the common sounds. For example, when the children indicate that the picture of a *sun* does not belong with *rat, fat,* and *mat,* say,

T: **Yes, *rat, fat,* and *mat* rhyme. They sound the same at the end.**

Use the alphabet cards and put the a and t cards on the table to show the children the letters that represent the common sounds.

See Lesson 20 for directions.

Teacher Notes for Lesson 40

Say-It-and-Move-It

If you are using two letter tiles with your children, try t and f tiles today. Remind them that they need to listen carefully for each of these sounds.

Letter Name and Sound Instruction

Sound Boards

Remember to have the sound boards ready for the children by placing the letters they will need for the lesson in the top pocket before the lesson begins.

LESSON 40

Say-It-and-Move-It

Materials: 1 *Say-It-and-Move-It* sheet per child
4 blank disks or tiles per child
1 disk or tile per child with <u>f</u>

Give children four blank tiles and a tile with <u>f</u>.

T: **Can you tell which sound we need to listen carefully for today? Yes. /f/.**

T: **Are you ready? Fingers in the air?**

fit
run
if
ten
is
fun
fib

Letter Name and Sound Instruction

Sound Boards

Materials: 1 sound board per child with <u>a</u>, <u>m</u>, <u>t</u>, <u>r</u>, and <u>f</u>

The children will need the <u>a</u>, <u>m</u>, <u>t</u>, <u>r</u>, and <u>f</u> letters in the top pocket of their sound boards. Review the name and sound of each letter.

Teacher Notes for Lesson 40

As in Lesson 39, this lesson uses a patterned sequence of word building that makes it easy to individualize instruction for children at different ability levels.

<u>a</u>	Ask a child who still needs review of single sounds to put the letter that makes the /a/ sound in the lower pocket.
am	Ask a child who is at a beginning word building level to make /a/ into *am.*
ram	Ask a higher level child to make *am* into *ram.*
rat	Ask the *highest* level child to make *ram* into *rat.* (If you don't have anyone who can do this yet, just show the children how to make *ram* into *rat* on your sound board and go on to the next word.)
fat	Ask another higher level child to make *rat* into *fat.*
at	Ask a child who is at a beginning word building level to take one letter away to make *fat* into *at.*
<u>a</u>	Ask a child who still needs review of single sounds to take one letter away from *at* to leave the letter that makes the /a/ sound.

OR

If your children are ready to build words with /i/, they will need the <u>i</u>, <u>t</u>, <u>f</u>, and <u>s</u> letters in the top pocket of their sound boards. Review the name and sound of each letter. Try using the following pattern: <u>i</u>, *it, fit, sit, it, if,* <u>i</u>.

Teacher Notes for Lesson 40

Phonological Awareness Practice

Phonological Awareness Practice

Post Office

Materials: Small alphabet picture cards of <u>a</u>, <u>m</u>, <u>t</u>, <u>i</u>, <u>s</u>, <u>r</u>, <u>b</u>, and <u>f</u>
Brown lunch bags
Pictures of objects that start with /a/, /m/, /t/, /i/,
/s/, /r/, /b/, and /f/
Large canvas or shopping bag

By this lesson you should have already made eight lunch bags
to use as "mailboxes," one for each of the following sounds: /a/,
/m/, /t/, /i/, /s/, /r/, /b/, and /f/. Choose the sounds that need
the most practice. You will probably want to use four to six bags.
Each child should get three or four pictures to deliver.

See Lesson 23 for directions.

Teacher Notes for Lesson 41

Say-It-and-Move-It

Letter Name and Sound Instruction

Concentration

If you played this memory game with your children in Lesson 30, then you have already made at least two copies of each of the small, plain alphabet cards for all of the letters except f̲. Now make multiple copies of f̲ to add to your game. You should have at least 16 cards, shuffled and arranged face down in four rows on the table in front of the children.

LESSON 41

Say-It-and-Move-It

Materials: 1 *Say-It-and-Move-It* sheet per child
4 blank disks or tiles per child
1 disk or tile per child with r

Give the children four blank tiles and a tile with r.

T: **Which sound do you think we need to listen carefully for today? Yes. /r/.**

T: **Are you ready? Fingers in the air?**

rug
red
is
rut
an
rob
rag

Letter Name and Sound Instruction

Concentration

Materials: Plain alphabet cards of a, m, t, i, s, r, b, and f
(multiple pairs, see **Teacher Notes**)

Play using the letters a, m, t, i, s, r, b, and f.

See Lesson 14 for directions.

Teacher Notes for Lesson 41

Phonological Awareness Practice

Phonological Awareness Practice

Save the Rabbit

Materials: Chalkboard or dry erase board
Chalk or appropriate markers
Small pieces of paper
Box or other container

Play using five of the eight sounds we have introduced in this program.

See Lesson 25 for directions.

Teacher Notes for Lesson 42

Say-It-and-Move-It

If you are using two letter tiles with your children, try <u>b</u> and <u>f</u> tiles today. Remind the children to listen carefully for each of these sounds.

LESSON 42

Say-It-and-Move-It

Materials: 1 *Say-It-and-Move-It* sheet per child
4 blank disks or tiles per child
1 disk or tile per child with <u>b</u>

Give the children four blank tiles and a tile with <u>b</u>.

T: **Which sound do you think we will be listening for today?**

T: **Yes. /b/.**

T: **Are you ready? Fingers in the air?**

bed
rob
sap
Al
bin
fib
fun
but

Teacher Notes for Lesson 42

Proper pacing is crucial!

Letter Name and Sound Instruction

Sound Boards

In this lesson, we have provided two lists of words using /i/. If it is more appropriate for your children to continue working on making words with /a/, stay with lists that use just that vowel. However, you may have children who find a carefully sequenced pattern using only one vowel too easy. If that is the case, create more challenging lists, such as *at, bat, rat, ram, rim, rib, fib,* and *fit*. Notice that we change only one sound (and one letter) at a time, and we ask the children, **"Show me how you change ____ into ____."** We want children to think about the phonological structure of the word and decide whether the first, last, or middle sound must change.

Remember to have the sound boards ready for the children by placing the letters they will need for the lesson in the top pocket before the lesson begins.

Phonological Awareness Practice

Let's Fish!

Remember that to play this game you need a pole with string and a magnet attached to it. You also need to put magnetic tape or a paper clip on each picture card.

Letter Name and Sound Instruction

Sound Boards

Materials: 1 sound board per child with t̲, i̲, s̲, and f̲

The children will need the letters t̲, i̲, s̲, and f̲ in the top pocket of their sound boards. Review the name and sound of each letter. If this is the first time you are introducing building words with /i/, try the following pattern: i̲, *it, fit, sit, it, if,* i̲.

If you used this pattern in Lesson 40 *and* if the children are ready to move on, try this pattern: i̲, *it, bit, fit, fib, rib,* i̲.

Remember, if you use this second list of words, the children will need to have the letters t̲, i̲, r̲, b̲, and f̲ in the top pocket of their sound boards.

Phonological Awareness Practice

Let's Fish!

Materials: Fishing pole
"Fish" representing each of the sounds that need to be reviewed

This is a good chance to work on the sounds that are still giving the children trouble. Choose the sounds that need the most practice and use pictures of objects (the "fish") that begin with those sounds.

See Lesson 15 for directions.

Teacher Notes for Lesson 43

Say-It-and-Move-It

If you are using two letter tiles with your children, try <u>t</u> and <u>i</u> tiles today. Remind the children to listen carefully for each of these sounds.

LESSON 43

Say-It-and-Move-It

Materials: 1 *Say-It-and-Move-It* sheet per child
4 blank disks or tiles per child
1 disk or tile per child with <u>i</u>

Give the children four blank tiles and a tile with <u>i</u>.

T: **Which sound do you think we will be listening for today?**

T: **Yes. /i/.**

T: **Are you ready? Fingers in the air?**

is
zip
lap
top
bit
fin
it
us

Teacher Notes for Lesson 43

Letter Name and Sound Instruction

Sound Boards

This is the last sound board activity, but we hope you won't put your boards away just because you have completed the program. Although we have restricted the letters used in the sound board activities in this program to only eight, we hope you will expand the sound board activities to include additional letters and sounds as your children learn them.

Letter Name and Sound Instruction

Sound Boards

Materials: 1 sound board per child with various letters
(see below)

Give your children sound boards that have the letters they will need for this lesson in the top pocket.

A. If your children have been using only words with /a/, you may either continue at that level (see Lessons 36, 37, 39, and 40 for lists with /a/) or use the first list of /i/ words for the sound board, presented in Lesson 40.

B. If your children have been successful with each of the previous Sound Board lessons, they may be ready to mix words with /a/ and /i/.

Try making the following words on the sound board:

at, mat, at, it, fit, sit, it

C. If your children are ready for a more advanced list, use the following pattern:

am, ram, rat, at, it, fit, fat

Teacher Notes for Lesson 43

Phonological Awareness Practice

Sound Categorization by Rhyme and Initial Sound

Today, when you use the Sound Categorization cards, select the *at* and *am* rhyming sets and the initial sound sets that use /b/ and /m/ in the initial position. You will also need the small, plain alphabet cards with the letters <u>a</u>, <u>m</u>, <u>t</u>, and <u>b</u> on them. As children group by rhyme or initial sound, use the alphabet cards to show them which letters the words have in common.

Phonological Awareness Practice

Sound Categorization by Rhyme and Initial Sound

Materials: *At* and *am* Sound Categorization by Rhyme cards
/b/ and /m/ Sound Categorization by Initial
Sound cards
Small, plain alphabet cards of <u>a</u>, <u>m</u>, <u>t</u>, and <u>b</u>

Repeat the sound categorization lesson described below (originally from Lesson 39) or select another phonological awareness activity that your children enjoy.

Select *at* and *am* rhyming sets and initial sound sets that you can group by /b/ and /m/. As the children identify the words that rhyme or begin the same, help them articulate the rule and identify the letters that represent the common sounds. For example, when the children indicate that the picture of a *sun* does not belong with *rat, fat,* and *mat,* say,

T: **Yes, *rat, fat,* and *mat* rhyme. They sound the same at the end.**

Use the alphabet cards and put the <u>a</u> and <u>t</u> cards on the table to show the children the letters that represent the common sounds.

Teacher Notes for Lesson 44

Say-It-and-Move-It

If you have not yet introduced letter tiles to your children, we hope you will consider extending this program beyond the 44 lessons we have presented. You might want to go back to Lesson 20 and gradually introduce letter tiles as described in Lessons 20 through 44.

LESSON 44

Say-It-and-Move-It

Materials: 1 *Say-It-and-Move-It* sheet per child
4 blank disks or tiles per child
1 disk or tile per child with f̲

Give the children four blank tiles and a tile with f̲.

T: **Which sound do you think we will be listening for today?**

T: **Yes. /f/.**

T: **Are you ready? Fingers in the air?**

fan
if
sun
fun
fit
tip
Ed

Teacher Notes for Lesson 44

Letter Name and Sound Instruction

Sound Bingo

You will need to photocopy from the **Materials Section** of the manual the Sound Bingo cards that reinforce a, i, r, b, and f. As always, there are five different cards for today's version of the game, so each child can have a different card.

Letter Name and Sound Instruction

Sound Bingo

Materials: 1 Sound Bingo card per child that reinforces <u>a</u>, <u>i</u>, <u>r</u>, <u>b</u>, and <u>f</u>

Copies of students' Sound Bingo cards, cut up and put in a box

1 handful of Bingo chips per child

1 die with letters on each side (for Option II)

Play using letters <u>a</u>, <u>i</u>, <u>r</u>, <u>b</u>, and <u>f</u>. You may use either Option I or Option II. If you are using Option II, the sixth side of the die may be designated as a "free call." This is how it works: Put a star (★) on the sixth side. If the child rolls a star, the child can call any letter or picture he or she chooses.

See Lesson 7 for directions.

The following pictures are on the Sound Bingo cards:

<u>a</u> **pictures**	<u>i</u> **pictures**	<u>r</u> **pictures**
ambulance	igloo	rabbit
ant	iguana	rain
apple	insects	reindeer
		runner

<u>b</u> **pictures**	<u>f</u> **pictures**
ballerina	feather
balloon	fish
bananas	football
bat and ball	Frankenstein
birthday cake	frog

Teacher Notes for Lesson 44

Phonological Awareness Practice

As the children learn additional sounds (beyond the eight sounds taught in these lessons), we hope you will add them to the games you have made for this program and continue to play the games with the children in your class.

Phonological Awareness Practice

Post Office

Materials: Small alphabet picture cards of <u>a</u>, <u>m</u>, <u>t</u>, <u>i</u>, <u>s</u>, <u>r</u>, <u>b</u>, and <u>f</u>
Brown lunch bags
Pictures of objects that start with /a/, /m/, /t/, /i/,
    /s/, /r/, /b/, and /f/
Large canvas or shopping bag

By this lesson you should have already made eight lunch bags
to use as "mailboxes," one for each of the following sounds: /a/,
/m/, /t/, /i/, /s/, /r/, /b/, and /f/. Choose the sounds that need
the most practice. You will probably want to use four to six bags.
Each child should get three or four pictures to deliver.

See Lesson 23 for directions.

Materials

Materials Provided

Say-It-And-Move-It Sheets
Jingles to Accompany Alphabet Cards
Large Alphabet Picture Cards
Small Alphabet Picture Cards
Small, Plain Alphabet Cards
Sound Categorization Cards
 By Rhyme
 By Initial Sound
Sound Bingo Cards
Elkonin Cards
Sound Board Instructions

Materials Not Provided

To use this program with your children, you will need to provide materials for the following games and activities:

Say-It-And-Move-It (at least one of the following)
- tiles
- disks
- wooden inch blocks
- buttons

Fix-It
- puppet with a mouth that opens and closes

Sound Bingo
- Bingo chips
- wooden inch block or die

Post Office
- paper lunch bags
- large canvas bag or shopping bag

Let's Fish!
- dowel with string and magnet attached
- magnetic tape or paper clips

List of Materials

Pictures of objects with the sounds of the eight letters introduced in this program (a, m, t, i, s, r, b, and f) are used in games and activities throughout this manual. As we suggest in the lessons, you can cut up the Sound Bingo cards and use the individual pictures for various games. You can also add to your collection of pictures by using published sets of consonant cards and using pictures cut out of magazines.

Say-It-and-Move-It

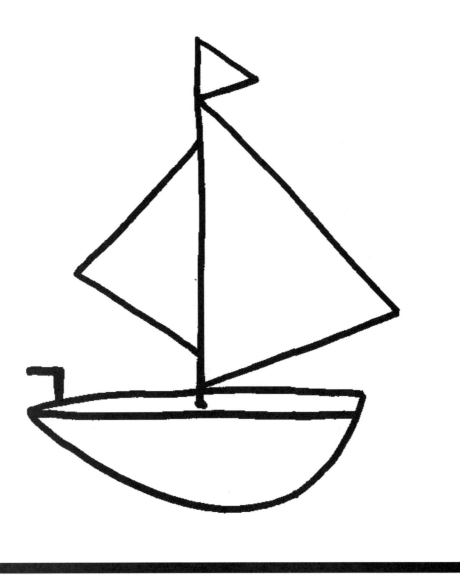

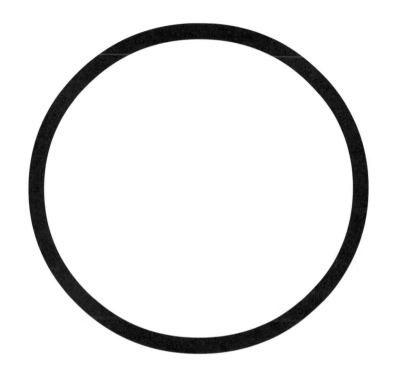

Jingles to Accompany Alphabet Cards

Jingles to Accompany Alphabet Cards

a   an apple and an ant
b   big boy bouncing on a bed
c   cool cat cooking cookies
d   dirty dog digging a deep ditch
e   Edwina (or Eddy) on the edge of an "E"
f   five funny faces
g   goofy goat golfing
h   Harry, the hip hippo, waves hello by his hut
i   itchy iguanas in an igloo
j   jackrabbit jumping over jars of jam
k   Katie the kangaroo (and her kid too)
l   leaping lizards licking lollipops
m   Mike the marvelous monkey
n   Nancy nibbles noodles and nuts
o   Ollie the olive octopus has an octagon
p   Peter the parrot pays for polka dot pajamas
q   quilting queens
r   red rooster in red running shoes
s   six silly snakes
t   two teenagers talking on the telephone
u   ugly umbrella going up
v   vampire with a violin
w   wagon with wobbly wheels
x   fo<u>x</u> in a bo<u>x</u>
y   yawning yellow yak
z   zebras with zippers

Large Alphabet Picture Cards

Large Alphabet Picture Cards

Large Alphabet Picture Cards

Large Alphabet Picture Cards

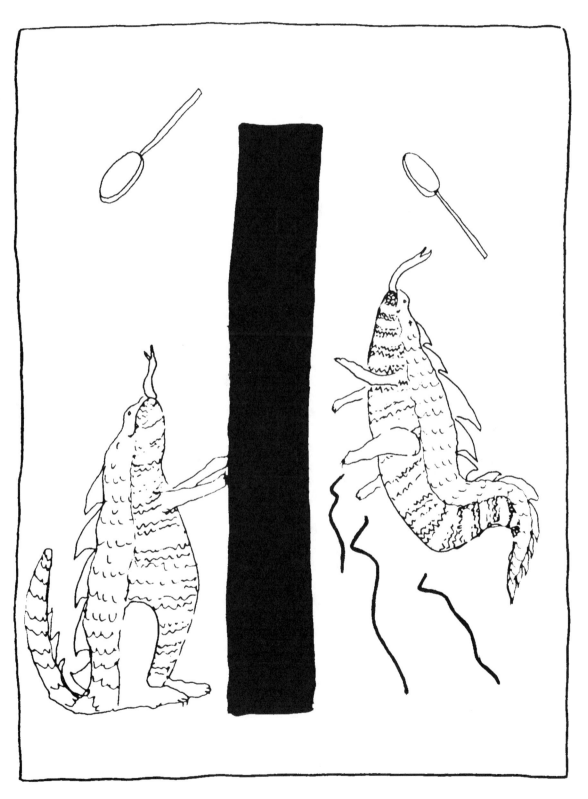

Large Alphabet Picture Cards

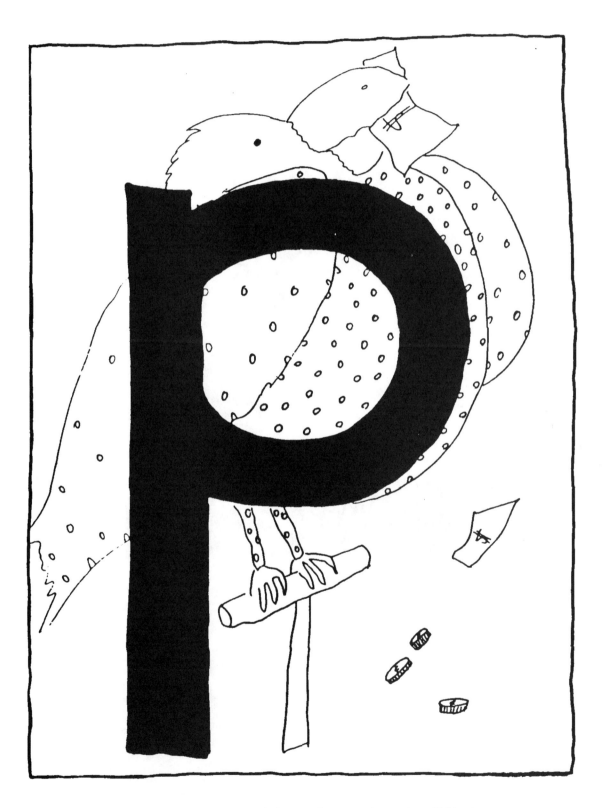

Large Alphabet Picture Cards

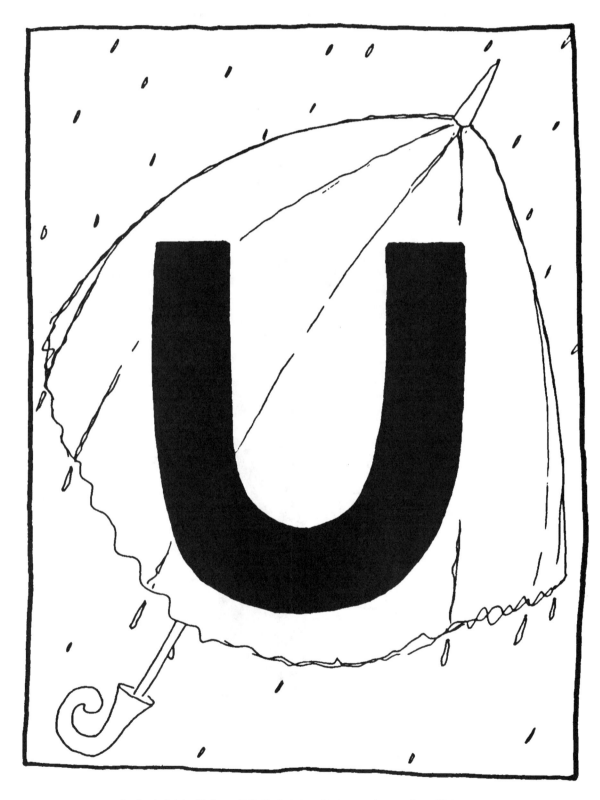

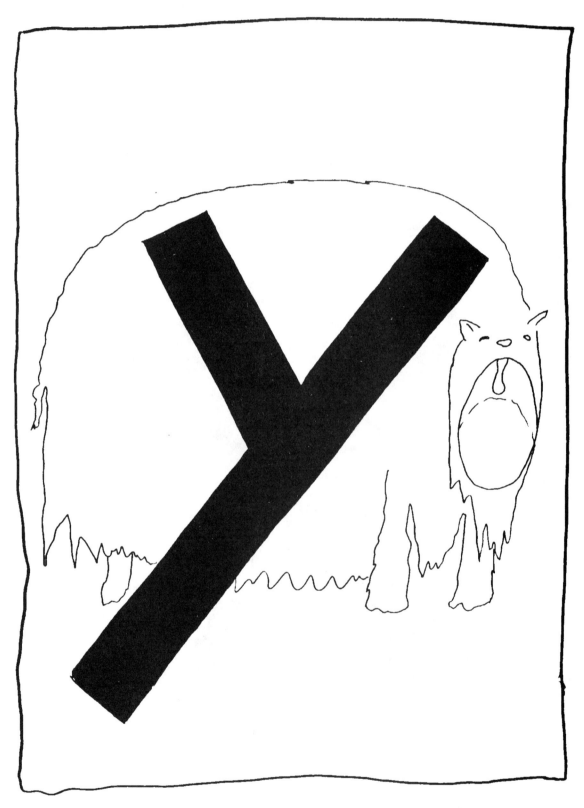

Small Alphabet Picture Cards

Road to the Code by Blachman, Ball, Black, & Tangel © 2000 Paul H. Brookes Publishing Co.

Small Alphabet Picture Cards

Small Alphabet Picture Cards

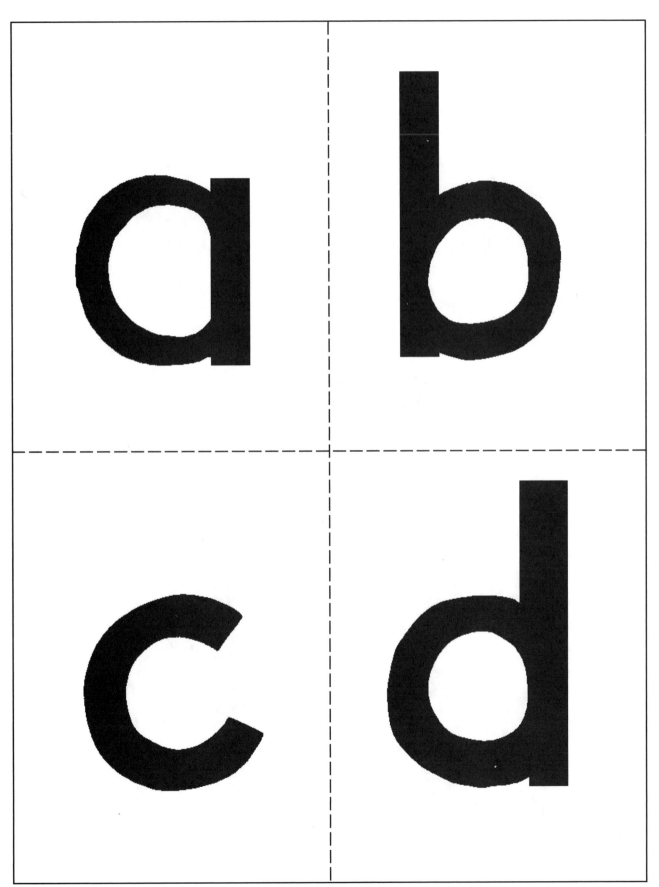

Small, Plain Alphabet Cards

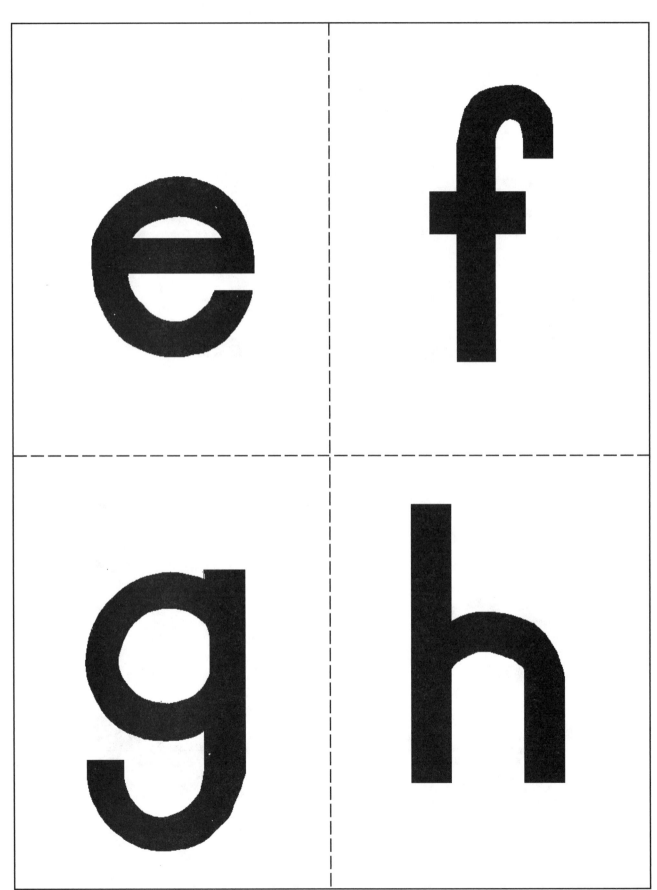

Road to the Code by Blachman, Ball, Black, & Tangel © 2000 Paul H. Brookes Publishing Co.

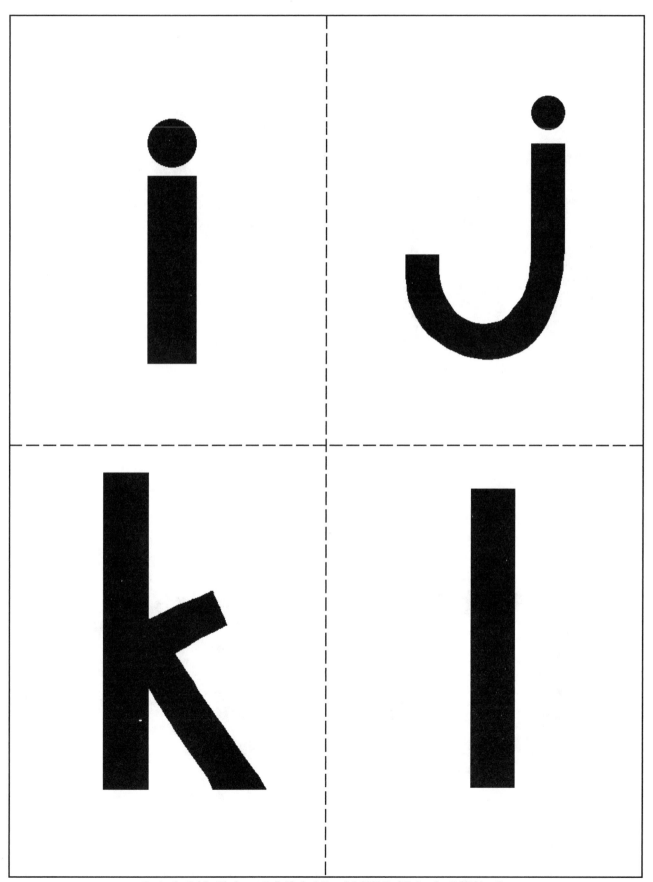

Small, Plain Alphabet Cards

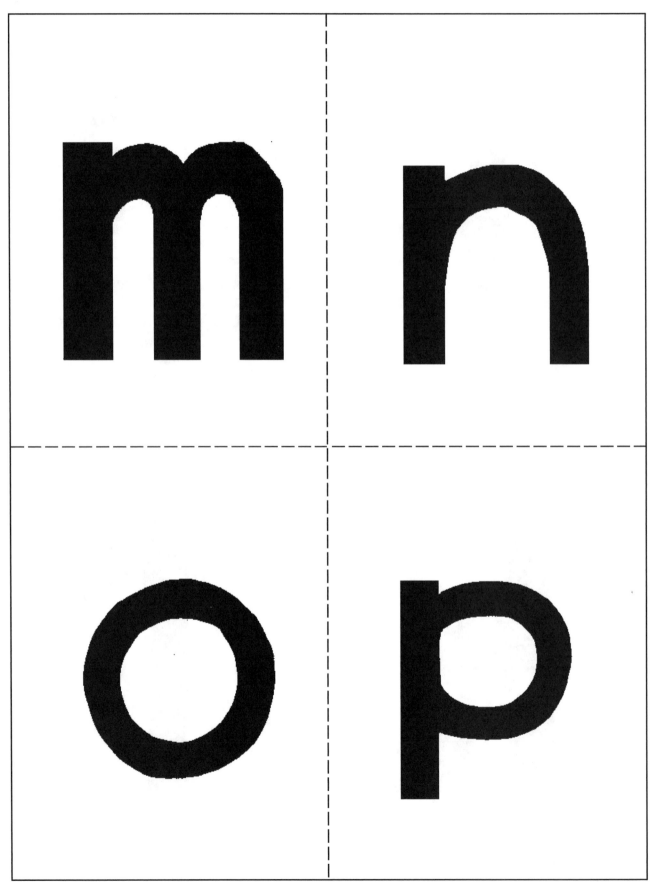

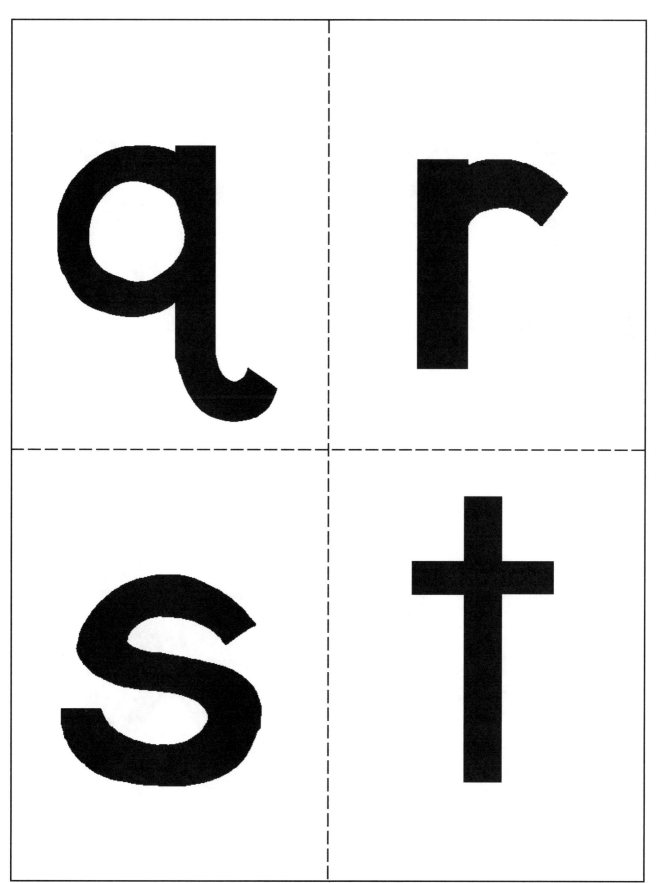

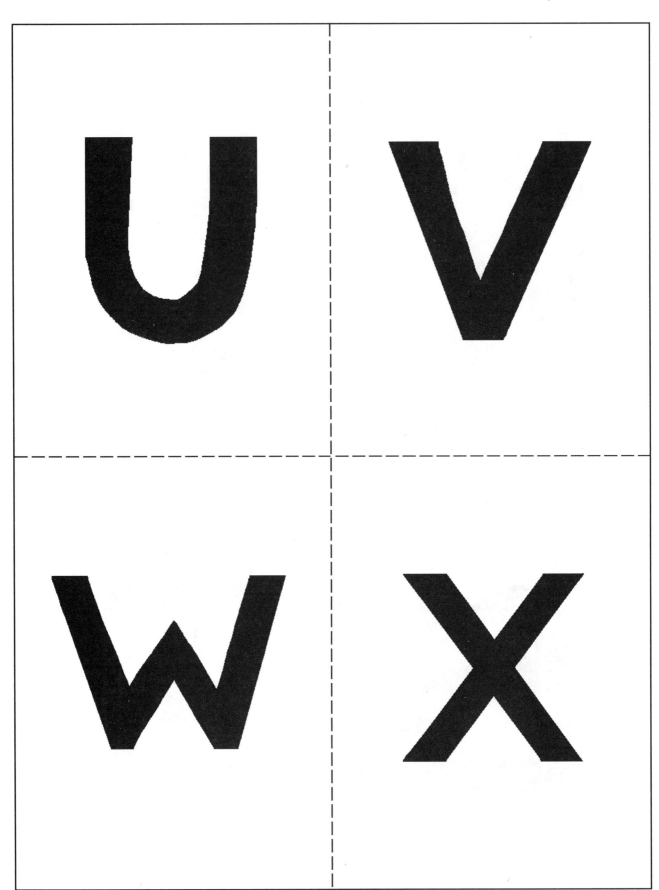

Road to the Code by Blachman, Ball, Black, & Tangel © 2000 Paul H. Brookes Publishing Co.

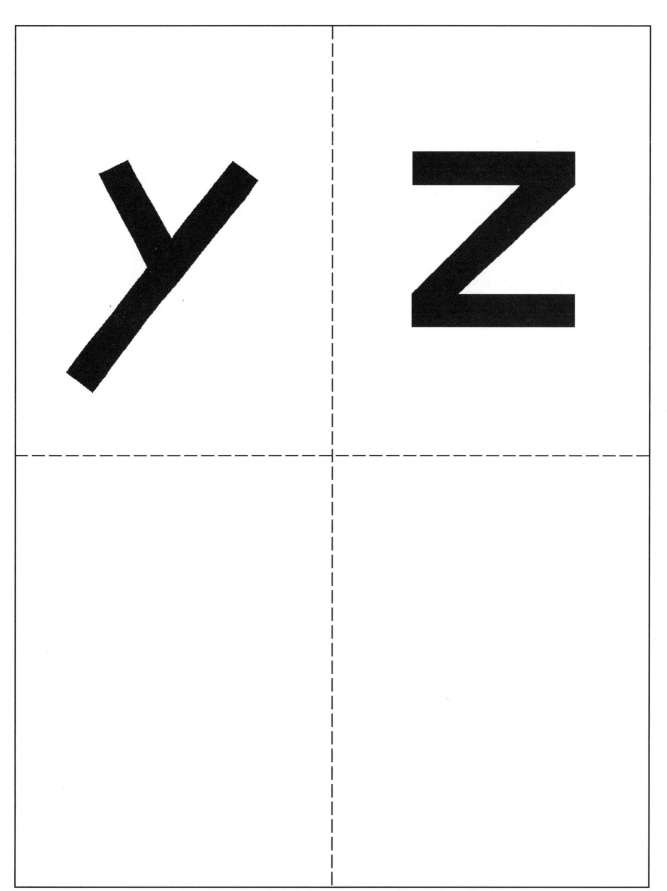

By Rhyme: pan   fan

can   bug

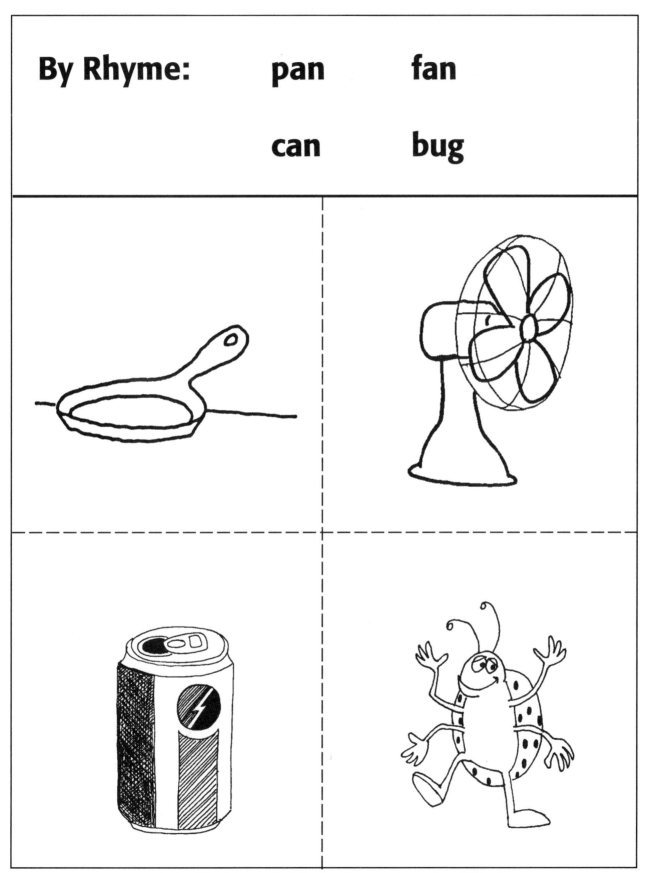

By Rhyme: net   hen

                          pen   ten

By Rhyme: fan   tug

bug   hug

Sound Categorization Cards

By Rhyme: sun fat

rat pat

By Rhyme: **sit**   **nut**

hut   **cut**

Sound Categorization Cards

By Rhyme:	**jug**	**bat**
	cat	**hat**

By Rhyme: top   sun

run   bun

Sound Categorization Cards

By Rhyme: **cut** **mop**

hop **top**

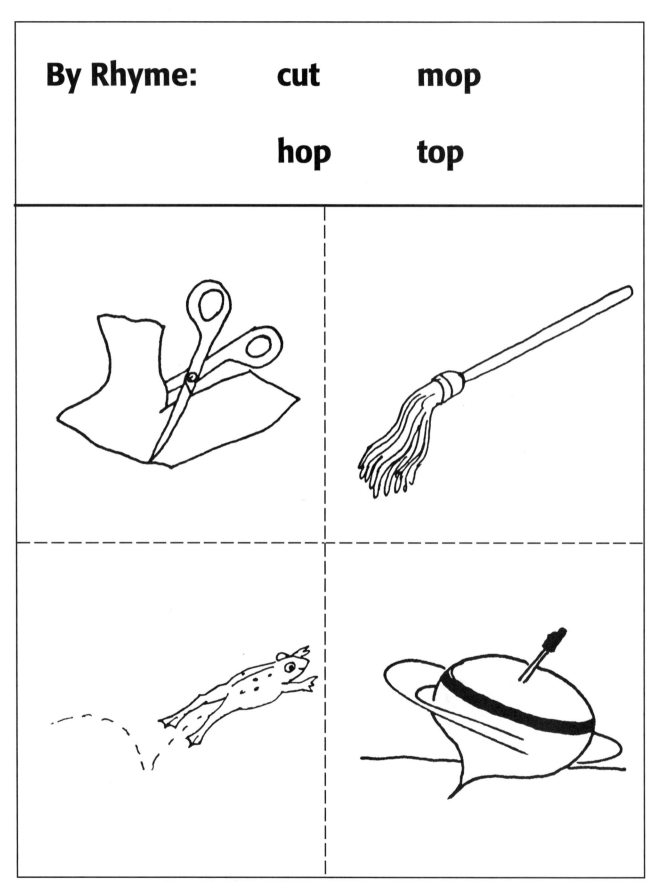

By Rhyme: **man**   **can**

                      pan   **nut**

Sound Categorization Cards

By Rhyme: mug   jug

tug   hop

By Rhyme: mat fan

hat cat

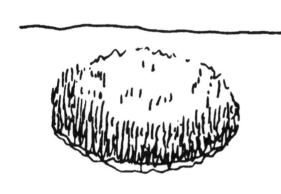

By Rhyme: cat   ram

jam   dam

By Initial Sound: pan pat

pin ram

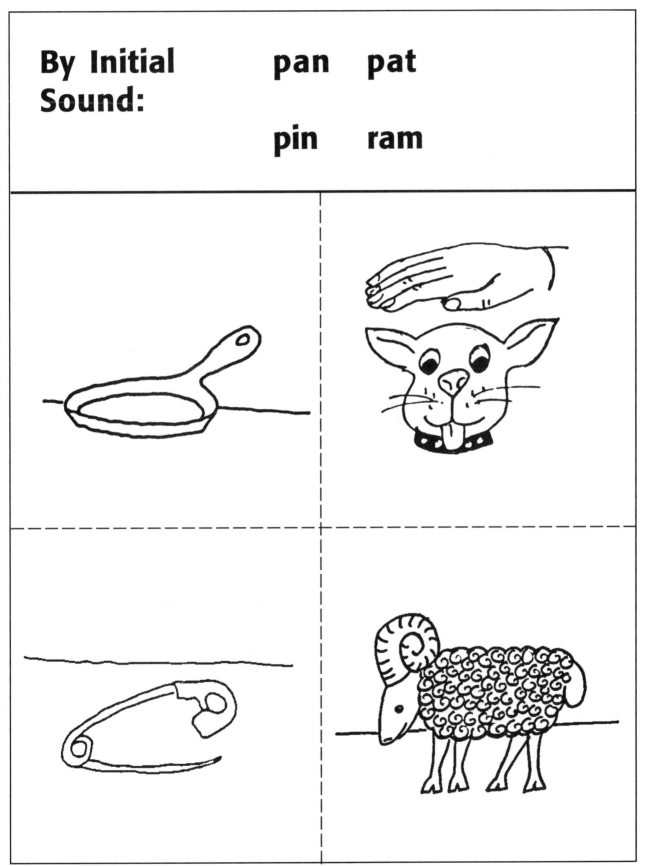

Sound Categorization Cards

By Initial Sound:	cab	ham
	hat	hot

Road to the Code by Blachman, Ball, Black, & Tangel © 2000 Paul H. Brookes Publishing Co.

By Initial Sound: cap   cup

cot   man

Sound Categorization Cards

By Initial Sound:	map	net
	nut	nun

By Initial Sound:	dot	jam
	jet	jug

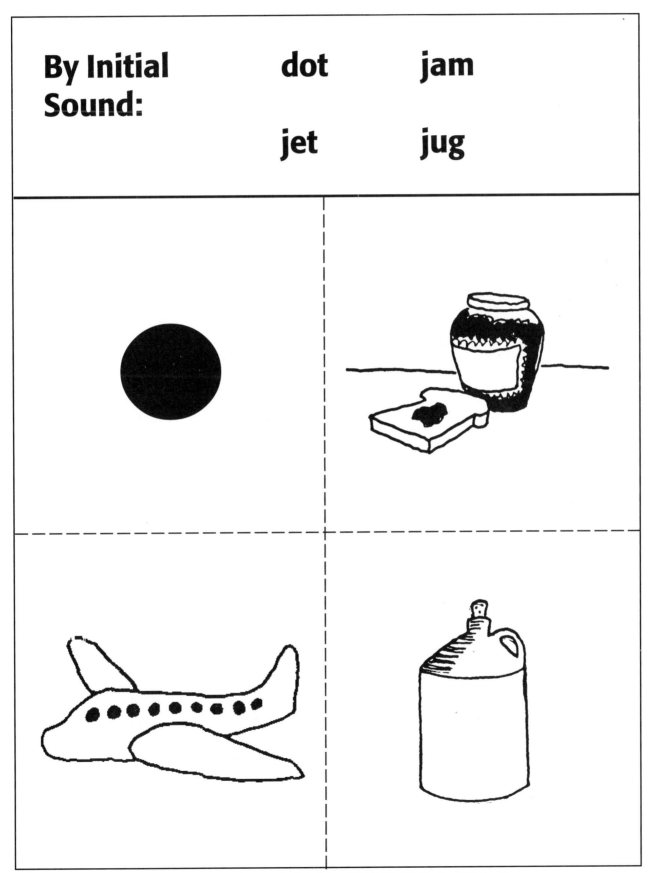

Sound Categorization Cards

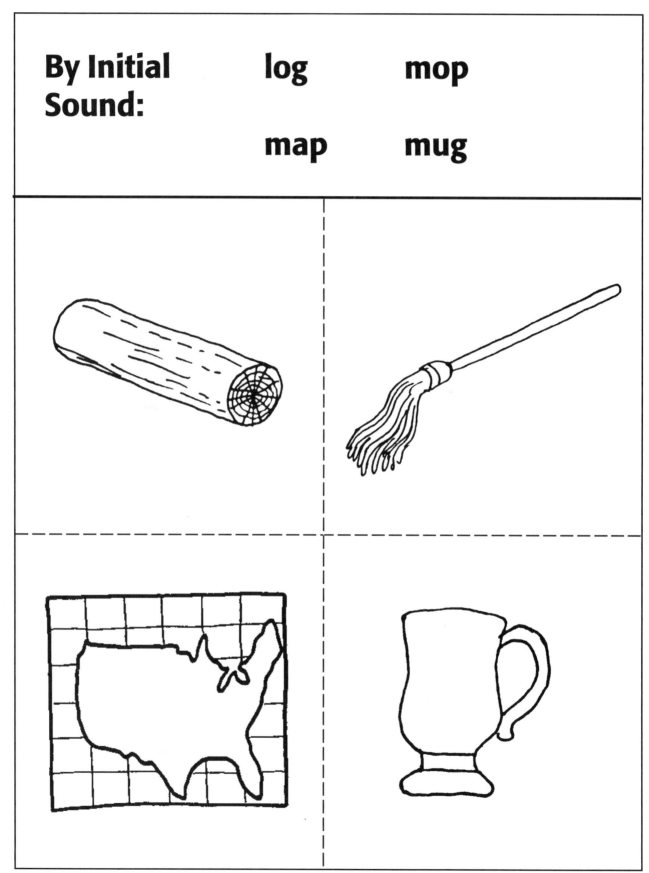

By Initial Sound:	log	mop
	map	mug

By Initial Sound: sit   bug

bun   bag

Sound Categorization Cards

By Initial Sound:	net	pig
	pot	pen

Road to the Code by Blachman, Ball, Black, & Tangel © 2000 Paul H. Brookes Publishing Co.

By Initial Sound: hen   map

hug   hut

Sound Categorization Cards

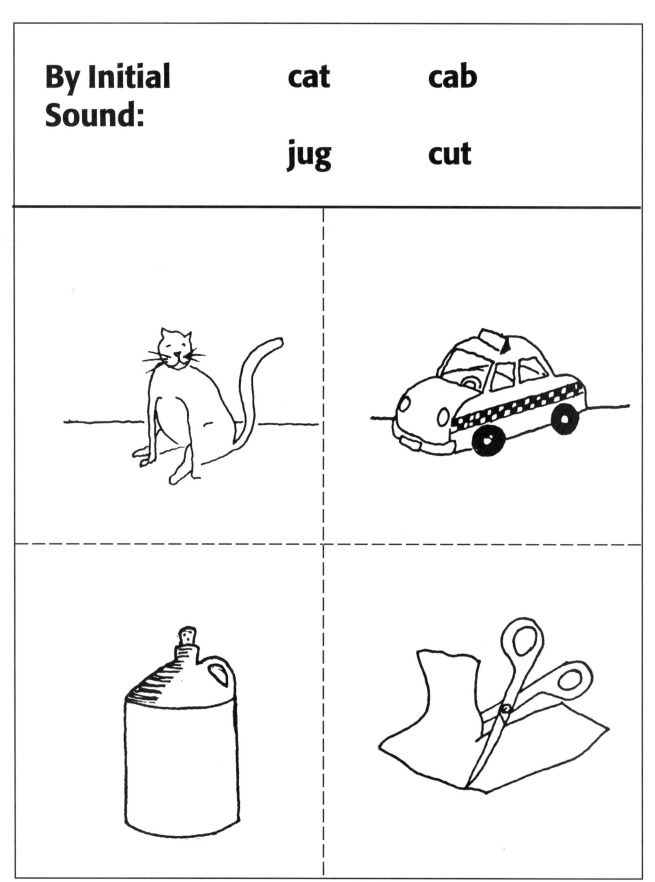

By Initial Sound:

cat   cab

jug   cut

By Initial Sound: **dig**   **dam**

                    dot   **bug**

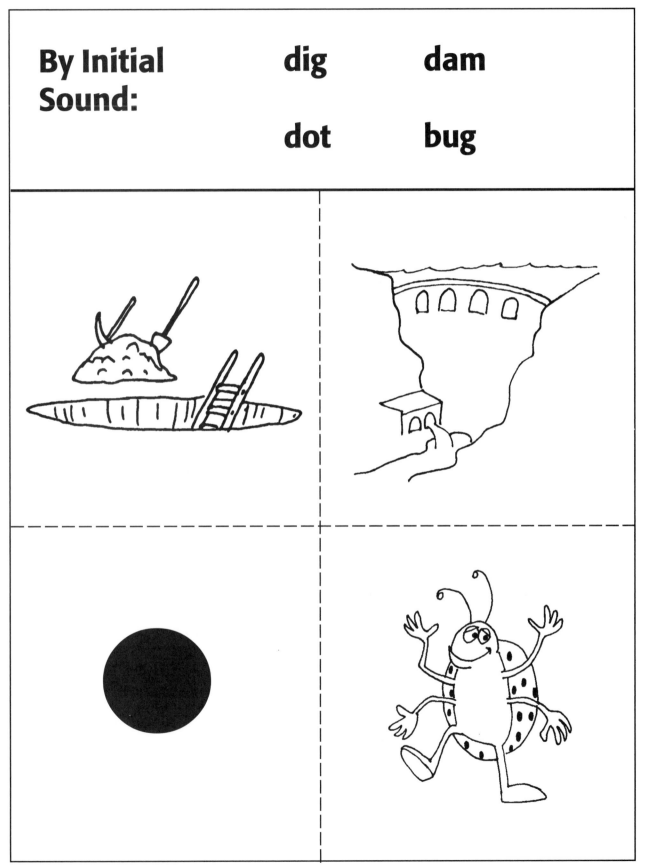

a/m

Sound Bingo Cards

a/m

Sound Bingo Cards

a/m

323

Sound Bingo Cards

a/m/t

Sound Bingo Cards

a/m/t

Sound Bingo Cards

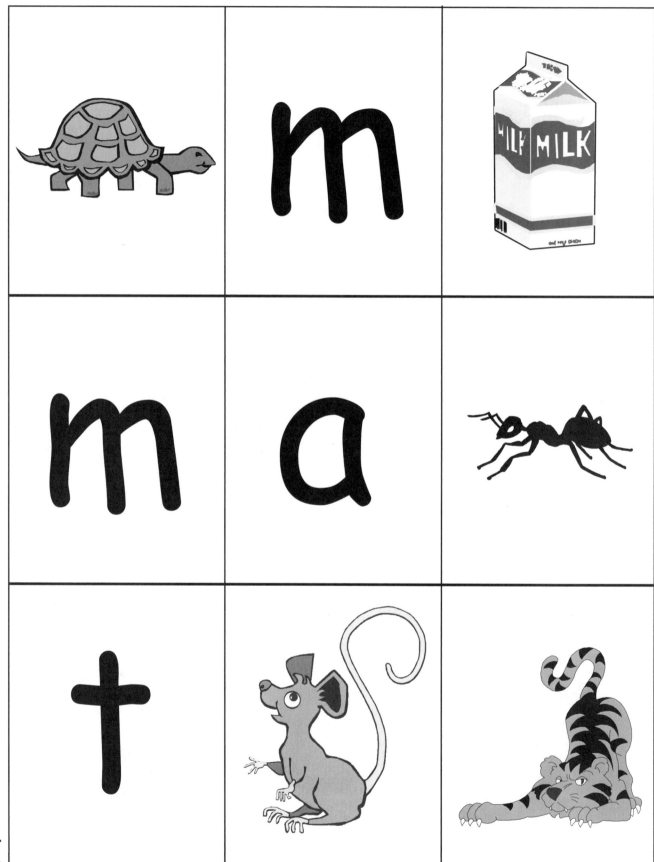

Sound Bingo Cards

a/m/t/i

Sound Bingo Cards

a/m/t/i

Sound Bingo Cards

a/m/t/i/s

335

Sound Bingo Cards

a/m/t/i/s

a/m/t/i/s

Sound Bingo Cards

a/m/t/i/s/r

Sound Bingo Cards

a/m/t/i/s/r

a/m/t/i/s/r

Sound Bingo Cards

a/m/t/i/s/r

a/m/t/i/s/r

Sound Bingo Cards

a/i/s/r/b

Sound Bingo Cards

a/i/s/r/b

Sound Bingo Cards

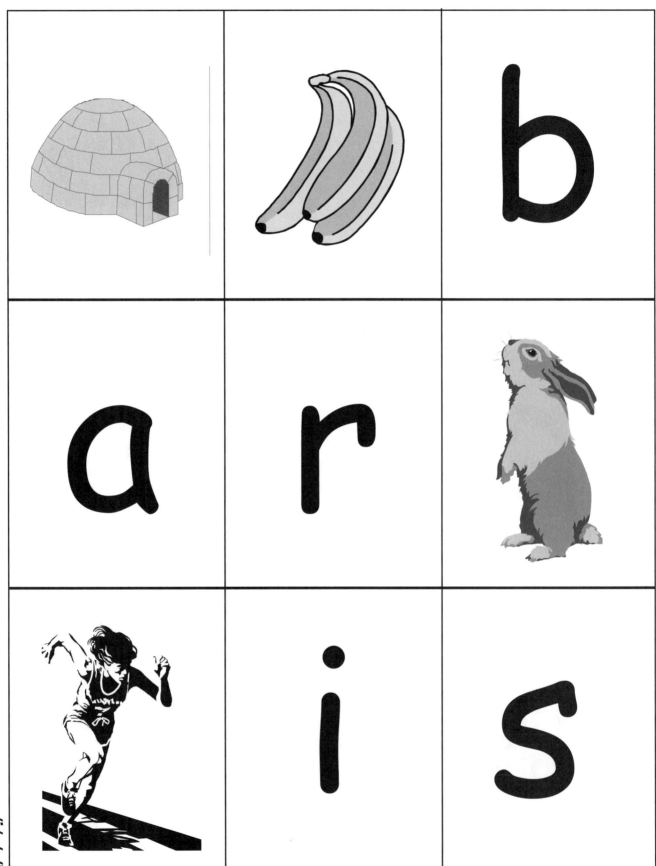

a/i/s/r/b

a/i/r/b/f

Sound Bingo Cards

Road to the Code by Blachman, Ball, Black, & Tangel © 2000 Paul H. Brookes Publishing Co.

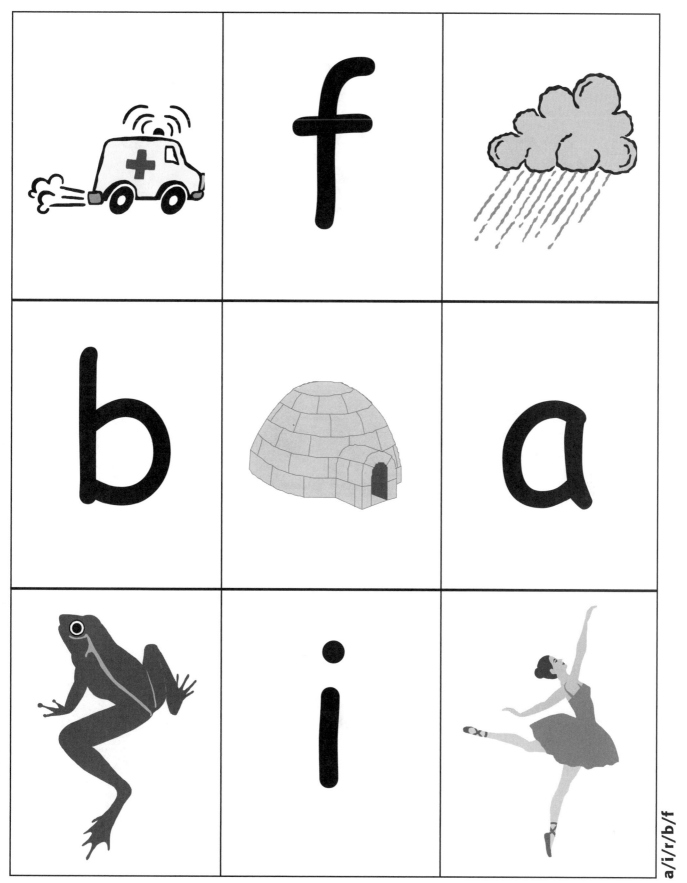

a/i/r/b/f

Sound Bingo Cards

a/i/r/b/f

a/i/r/b/f

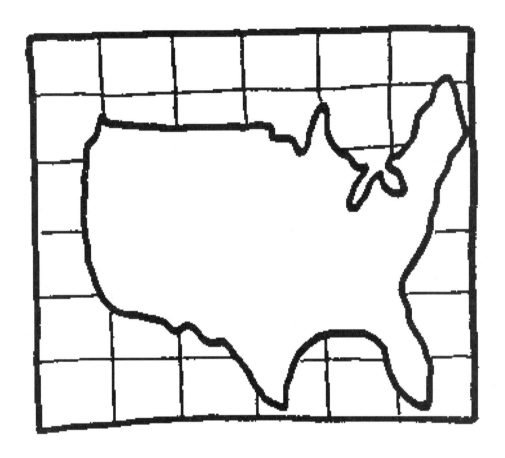

Elkonin Cards

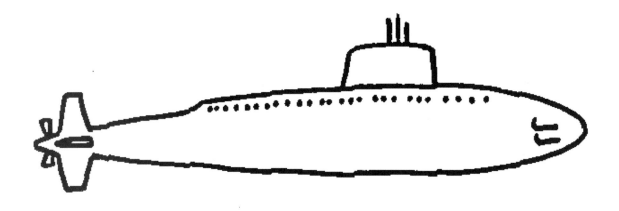

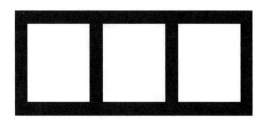

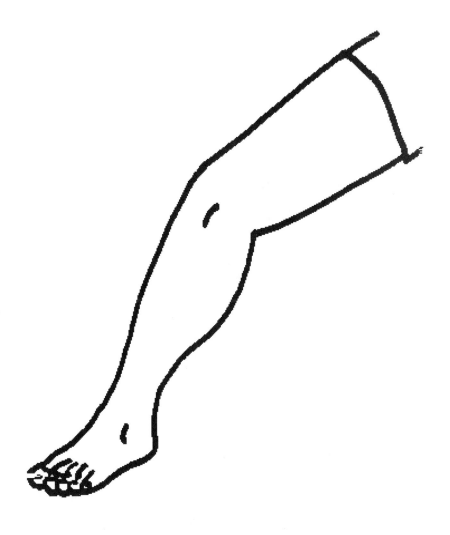

Elkonin Cards

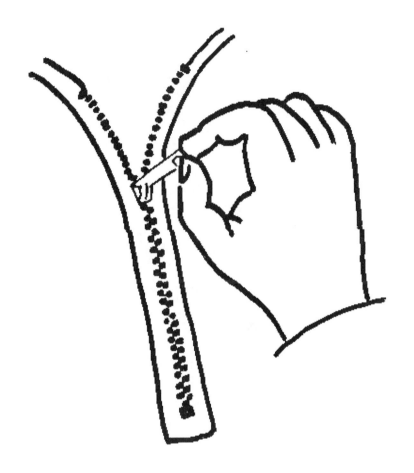

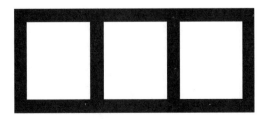

Elkonin Cards

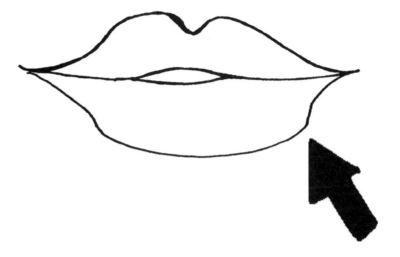

Elkonin Cards

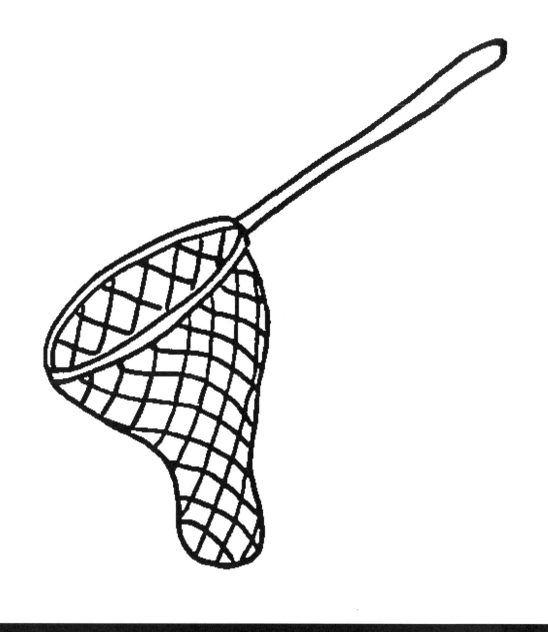

Elkonin Cards

Elkonin Cards

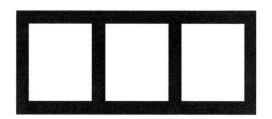

Elkonin Cards

Elkonin Cards

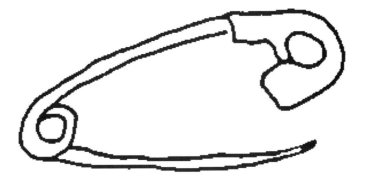

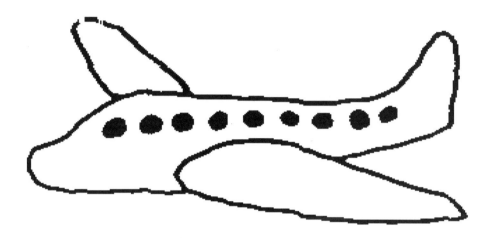

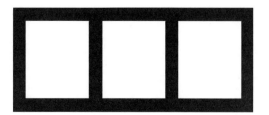

Elkonin Cards

Elkonin Cards

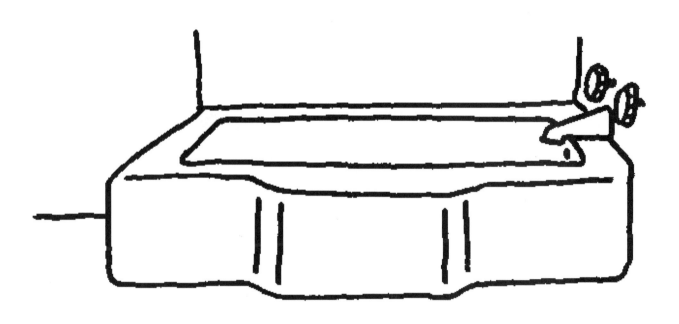

Elkonin Cards

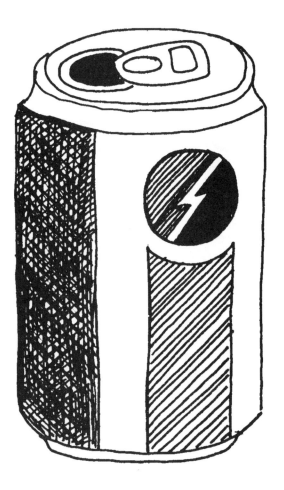

10

Directions for Making Sound Boards and Letter Cards

Materials

Poster board
Scotch 1.5-inch colored plastic tape
Red and black fine point markers
6 × 9 inch clasp envelopes

Directions

Sound Board:

1. Cut the poster board so that it measures 8.5 inches by 11 inches.
2. Each sound board should have two strips 1.5 inches wide to form pockets for holding the letter cards. The strips should be a different color than the background.
3. Tape the strips with colored plastic tape across the bottom and lap the ends of the tape over to the back. Tape the entire perimeter of the board with the tape as well.

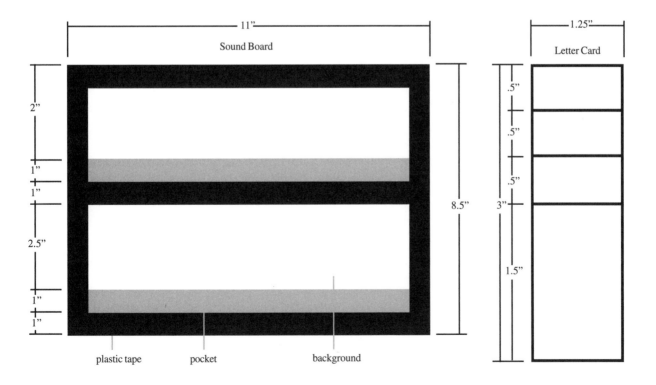

Sound Board Instructions

Letter Cards:
1. Letter cards should be white poster board cut into strips 1.25 inches wide and 3 inches long.
2. Individual letters should be printed on the top half of the cards so when the cards are inserted into the pockets the letters are lined up evenly.
3. The top half should be split into three .5 inch sections (see diagram). Use these sections as a guide to help you space the letters evenly. For example, use the middle section when writing the letter <u>a</u> and use the middle and upper section when writing the letter <u>b</u>. As you add more letters to the sound board (beyond the eight letters introduced in this program), you will use the middle and lower section to write the letter <u>p</u>, for example.
4. Consonants should be written in black and vowels in red.
5. On the back of the sound board, tape a 6 × 9 inch clasp envelope to hold the letter cards not in use.

Frequently Asked Questions

Q: **Why do you use only closed syllables?**

A: Throughout this program we use words that represent only one syllable pattern—the closed syllable. In a closed syllable word, such as *at* or *rip,* there is only one vowel and the word ends in a consonant. Closed syllables often end in more than one consonant, as in *camp* or *splash;* however, for this program we have elected to use only closed syllables that end in a single consonant. The other consistent characteristic is that the vowel sound in a closed syllable is short. These short vowel sounds are listed below:

> **a** as in <u>a</u>pple, animal
> **i** as in <u>i</u>gloo, itch
> **o** as in <u>o</u>ctopus, olive
> **u** as in <u>u</u>mbrella, ugly
> **e** as in <u>e</u>dge, Ed

Because we are working just with closed syllables, children need to learn the sounds of the short vowels. We introduce two of these sounds (the short sounds of **a** as in *apple* and **i** as in *igloo*) during the letter sound instruction portion of the program. We also introduce the sounds of six consonants, specifically the sounds of **m**, **t**, **s**, **r**, **b**, and **f**. We recommend that you teach the other consonants and the other short vowel sounds in kindergarten or at whatever time children become ready for the instructional activities introduced in this program.

We emphasize closed syllables because learning to segment closed syllables (e.g., learning to move disks to represent the three phonemes in the spoken word "sun") makes it especially easy for children to make the transition later to reading and spelling closed syllable words. If you understand that the word *sun* has three parts, it is easier to understand how alphabetic transcription works and thus easier to understand why *sun* is written with three letters. Learning to read and spell closed syllable words is not one of the primary instructional goals for this program. However, from the foun-

Frequently Asked Questions

dation children get with this program, they can go on to learn to read and spell closed syllable words—followed by the other five syllable patterns—when they get to more formal reading instruction. The other syllable patterns include open syllables (e.g., *he, go*), final e syllables (e.g., *lake, slope*), vowel team syllables (e.g., *rain, oat, spoil*), vowel + r syllables (e.g., *car, perch, storm*), and consonant + le syllables (e.g., *handle, noble*).

Q: **Why do you use *at* but not *of* or *add*?**

A: We've been very selective about the two-phoneme words we have elected to use. We didn't use *of* and *add,* for example, even though both have two phonemes. The sound of the o in *of* is not phonetically regular. If the word *of* was phonetically regular, the o would have the sound that one hears at the beginning of *octopus*. In this program we use only phonetically regular words.

We didn't use words like *add* because, even though *add* has two phonemes and is phonetically regular, the conventional spelling has three letters. You might wonder why we are concerned about the spelling of a word, since children don't see the words during the segmentation activities (these are all oral language activities). We chose to use only words where the number of sounds corresponds to the number of letters because we felt consistency would facilitate teacher planning.

As children develop conventional spelling, it is important for them to understand that some sounds must be represented in print by two letters (e.g., *ebb, pain*). However, in this program, our goals are simply to have children understand that spoken words can be segmented into phonemes and that the segmented units can be represented by single letters. Understanding that sometimes these segments need to be represented by more than one letter comes later in the developmental progression, as students learn more about orthographic patterns and conventional spelling through exposure to print and experience with writing.

Frequently Asked Questions

Q: **Why do you use *lap* but not *last?***

A: In this program we have also chosen not to use words with more than three phonemes. We stayed with three-phoneme words, as opposed to four- or five-phoneme words, such as *last* or *splat,* because we feel that developing phonological insight with three-phoneme words is adequate at this age and developmental level. However, it might be helpful to use four- and five-phoneme words with older children who are receiving remedial instruction because it provides them with more challenging words and a deeper insight about the phonological structure of words.

Q: **How did you decide that Post Office, for example, is a phonological awareness activity, while Sound Bingo is a letter name and sound activity?**

A: In some cases we made a somewhat arbitrary decision about whether to list an activity under *Phonological Awareness Practice* or under *Letter Name and Sound Instruction.* Many activities to teach letter sounds, for example, require the isolation of the first sound in the word. Such activities could be included under either *Phonological Awareness Practice* or under *Letter Name and Sound Instruction.* Other activities fall more naturally in one category or the other, such as our sound categorization activities (rhyming and initial sound) that we include under *Phonological Awareness Practice.*

Q: **Do the words in the *Say-It-and-Move-It* portion of the lesson have to contain the sounds that are being taught during *Letter Name and Sound Instruction?***

A: No. In fact, it is important to remember that *Say-It-and-Move-It* is about segmenting the sounds in spoken words. It is an oral language activity and does not require that children identify the specific letters that make those sounds. Therefore, we can use words during *Say-It-and-Move-It* that include sounds which are not being taught during the letter sound portion of these lessons. Even though we don't expect the children at this point to be able to tell you, for example, what two letters are in *up,* they should be able to tell you (and show you by moving disks to represent each sound) that *up* has two parts.

Q: **Can this program be used for remediation with older children who are still at this early stage of reading development?**

A: Yes and no. The concepts taught in these lessons need to be understood by students of any age who are learning to read. However, the majority of materials provided in this program to teach these concepts would not be appropriate, because they were developed to appeal to younger children. We have worked with many creative teachers who have found ways to develop more sophisticated materials that appeal to an older audience. You might, for example, want the older student to create alphabet pictures and jingles that have personal interest. Scrabble tiles can also be used to develop phoneme awareness and letter sound knowledge with older students.

References and Suggested Readings

Adams, M.J. (1990). *Beginning to read: Thinking and learning about print.* Cambridge: M.I.T. Press.

Adams, M.J., Foorman, B.R., Lundberg, I., & Beeler, T. (1998). The elusive phoneme. *American Educator, 22*(1 & 2), 18–29.

Ball, E.W. (1993). Assessing phoneme awareness. *Language, Speech, and Hearing Services in Schools, 24,* 130–139.

Ball, E.W. (1997). Phonological awareness: Implications for whole language and emergent literacy programs. *Topics in Language Disorders, 17*(3), 14–26.

Ball, E.W., & Blachman, B.A. (1988). Phoneme segmentation training: Effect on reading readiness. *Annals of Dyslexia, 38,* 208–225.

Ball, E.W., & Blachman, B.A. (1991). Does phoneme awareness training in kindergarten make a difference in early word recognition and developmental spelling? *Reading Research Quarterly, 26*(1), 49–66.

Blachman, B.A. (1987). An alternative classroom reading program for learning disabled and other low-achieving children. In R. Bowler (Ed.), *Intimacy with language: A forgotten basic in teacher education* (pp. 49–55). Baltimore: Orton Dyslexia Society.

Blachman, B.A. (1997). Early intervention and phonological awareness: A cautionary tale. In B.A. Blachman (Ed.), *Foundations of reading acquisition and dyslexia: Implications for early intervention* (pp. 409–430). Mahwah, NJ: Lawrence Erlbaum Associates.

Blachman, B.A. (2000). Phonological awareness. In M.L. Kamil, P.B. Mosenthal, P.D. Pearson, & R. Barr (Eds.), *Handbook of reading research* (Vol. III, pp. 483–502). Mahwah, NJ: Lawrence Erlbaum Associates.

Blachman, B.A., Ball, E.W., Black, R.S., & Tangel, D.M. (1994). Kindergarten teachers develop phoneme awareness in low-income, inner-city classrooms: Does it make a difference? *Reading and Writing: An Interdisciplinary Journal, 6,* 1–17.

References and Suggested Readings

Blachman, B.A., Tangel, D.M., Ball, E.W., Black, R., & McGraw, C.K. (1999). Developing phonological awareness and word recognition skills: A two-year intervention with low-income, inner-city children. *Reading and Writing: An Interdisciplinary Journal, 11,* 239–273.

Bradley, L., & Bryant, P. (1983). Categorizing sounds and learning to read: A causal connection. *Nature, 30,* 419–421.

Brady, S.A., & Shankweiler, D.P. (Eds.). (1991). *Phonological processes in literacy: A tribute to Isabelle Y. Liberman.* Mahwah, NJ: Lawrence Erlbaum Associates.

Bruck, M. (1992). Persistence of dyslexics' phonological awareness deficits. *Developmental Psychology, 28,* 874–886.

Bryant, P.E., Maclean, M., Bradley, L.L., & Crossland, J. (1990). Rhyme and alliteration, phoneme detection, and learning to read. *Developmental Psychology, 26,* 429–438.

Byrne, B., & Fielding-Barnsley, R. (1991). Evaluation of a program to teach phonemic awareness to young children. *Journal of Educational Psychology, 83,* 451–455.

Byrne, B., & Fielding-Barnsley, R. (1995). Evaluation of a program to teach phonemic awareness to young children: A 2- and 3-year follow-up and a new preschool trial. *Journal of Educational Psychology, 87,* 488–503.

Cary, L., & Verhaeghe, A. (1994). Promoting phonemic analysis ability among kindergartners: Effects of different training programs. *Reading and Writing: An Interdisciplinary Journal, 6,* 251–278.

Catts, H.W., & Kamhi, A.G. (Eds.). (1999). *Language and reading disabilities.* Needham Heights, MA: Allyn & Bacon.

Cunningham, A.E. (1990). Explicit versus implicit instruction in phonemic awareness. *Journal of Experimental Child Psychology, 50,* 429–444.

Ehri, L.C. (l998). Grapheme-phoneme knowledge is essential for learning to read words in English. In J. Metsala & L. Ehri (Eds.), *Word recognition in beginning literacy* (pp. 3–40). Mahwah, NJ: Lawrence Erlbaum Associates.

References and Suggested Readings

Elkonin, D.B. (1963). The psychology of mastering the elements of reading. In B. Simon & J. Simon (Eds.), *Educational psychology in the U.S.S.R.* London: Routledge Ltd.

Elkonin, D.B. (1973). U.S.S.R. In J. Downing (Ed.), *Comparative reading.* New York: Macmillan.

Fletcher, J.M., & Lyon, G.R. (1998). Reading: A research-based approach. In W.M. Evers (Ed.), *What's gone wrong in America's classrooms?* (pp. 50–90). Palo Alto, CA: Stanford University, Hoover Institution Press.

Fowler, A.E. (1991). How early phonological development might set the stage for phoneme awareness. In S.A. Brady & D.P. Shankweiler (Eds.), *Phonological processes in literacy: A tribute to Isabelle Y. Liberman* (pp. 97–117). Mahwah, NJ: Lawrence Erlbaum Associates.

Hoien, T., Lundberg, I., Stanovich, K.E., & Bjaalid, I. (1995). Components of phonological awareness. *Reading and Writing: An Interdisciplinary Journal, 7,* 171–188.

Juel, C. (1994). *Learning to read and write in one elementary school.* New York: Springer-Verlag.

Liberman, A.M., Cooper, F.S., Shankweiler, D.P., & Studdert-Kennedy, M. (1967). Perception of the speech code. *Psychological Review, 74,* 431–461.

Liberman, I.Y. (1973). Segmentation of the spoken word and reading acquisition. *Bulletin of the Orton Society, 23,* 65–67.

Liberman, I.Y., & Shankweiler, D. (1991). Phonology and beginning reading: A tutorial. In L. Rieben & C.A. Perfetti (Eds.), *Learning to read: Basic research and its implications* (pp. 3–17). Mahwah, NJ: Lawrence Erlbaum.

Liberman, I.Y., Shankweiler, D., Fischer, F.W., & Carter, B. (1974). Explicit syllable and phoneme segmentation in the young child. *Journal of Experimental Child Psychology, 18,* 201–212.

Lundberg, I., Frost, J., & Petersen, O. (1988). Effects of an extensive program for stimulating phonological awareness in preschool children. *Reading Research Quarterly, 23*(3), 263–284.

Moats, L.C. (1995). The missing foundation in teacher preparation. *American Educator, 19*(9), 43–51.

References and Suggested Readings

Murray, B.A., Stahl, S.A., & Ivey, M.G. (1996). Developing phoneme awareness through alphabet books. *Reading and Writing: An Interdisciplinary Journal, 8,* 307–322.

Nation, K., & Hulme, C. (1997). Phonemic segmentation, not onset-rime segmentation, predicts early reading and spelling skills. *Reading Research Quarterly, 32,* 154–167.

O'Connor, R.E., Jenkins, J.R., & Slocum, T.A. (1995). Transfer among phonological tasks in kindergarten: Essential instructional content. *Journal of Educational Psychology, 87,* 202–217.

O'Connor, R.E., Notari-Syverson, A., & Vadasy, P.F. (1996). Ladders to literacy: The effects of teacher-led phonological activities for kindergarten children with and without disabilities. *Exceptional Children, 63*(1), 117–130.

Scarborough, H.S. (1998). Early identification of children at risk for reading disabilities: Phonological awareness and some other promising predictors. In P. Accardo, A. Capute, & B. Shapiro (Eds.), *Specific reading disability: A view of the spectrum* (pp. 75–107). Timonium, MD: York Press.

Snider, V. (1995). A primer on phonemic awareness: What it is, why it's important, and how to teach it. *School Psychology Review, 24,* 443–455.

Snow, C.E., Burns, M.S., & Griffin, P. (Eds.). (1998). *Preventing reading difficulties in young children.* Washington, DC: National Academy Press.

Stahl, S.A., & Murray, B.A. (1994). Defining phonological awareness and its relationship to early reading. *Journal of Educational Psychology, 86,* 221–234.

Stanovich, K.E. (1986). Matthew effects in reading: Some consequences of individual differences in the acquisition of literacy. *Reading Research Quarterly, 21,* 360–407.

Stanovich, K.E. (1994). Romance and reality. *The Reading Teacher, 47,* 280–291.

Stanovich, K.E., Cunningham, A.E., & Cramer, B.B. (1984). Assessing phonological awareness in kindergarten children: Issues of task comparability. *Journal of Experimental Child Psychology, 38,* 175–190.

References and Suggested Readings

Tangel, D.M., & Blachman, B.A. (1992). Effect of phoneme awareness instruction on kindergarten children's invented spelling. *Journal of Reading Behavior, 24,* 233–261.

Tangel, D.M., & Blachman, B.A. (1995). Effect of phoneme awareness instruction on the invented spelling of first grade children: A one year follow-up. *Journal of Reading Behavior, 27,* 153–185.

Torgesen, J.K., & Burgess, S.R. (1998). Consistency of reading-related phonological processes throughout early childhood: Evidence from longitudinal, correlational and instructional studies. In J. Metsala & L. Ehri (Eds.), *Word recognition in beginning literacy* (pp. 161–188). Mahwah, NJ: Lawrence Erlbaum Associates.

Torgesen, J.K., & Mathes, P.G. (1998). *What every teacher should know about phonological awareness* (Technical Assistance Report). Tallahassee: Florida Department of Education.

Torgesen, J.K., Morgan, S.T., & Davis, C. (1992). Effects of two types of phonological awareness training on word learning in kindergarten children. *Journal of Educational Psychology, 84,* 364–370.

Vellutino, F.R., & Scanlon, D.M. (1987). Phonological coding, phonological awareness, and reading ability: Evidence from a longitudinal and experimental study. *Merrill-Palmer Quarterly, 33*(3), 321–363.

Vellutino, F.R., Scanlon, D.M., Sipay, E.R., Small, S.G., Pratt, A., Chen, R.S., & Denckla, M.B. (1996). Cognitive profiles of difficult to remediate and readily remediated poor readers: Early intervention as a vehicle for distinguishing between cognitive and experiential deficits as basic causes of specific reading disability. *Journal of Educational Psychology, 88*(4), 607–638.

Williams, J.P. (1980). Teaching decoding with an emphasis on phoneme analysis and phoneme blending. *Journal of Educational Psychology, 72,* 1–15.

Yopp, H.K. (1995). A test for assessing phonemic awareness in young children. *The Reading Teacher, 49,* 20–29.